LET'S LAUGH!

Discovering How Laughter
Will Make You Healthy

C. Peter Wagner

Destiny Image® Publishers, Inc.
P.O. Box 310
Shippensburg, PA 17257-0310

*"Speaking to the Purposes of God for this Generation
and for the Generations to Come."*

For Worldwide Distribution, Printed in the U.S.A.

ISBN 10: 0-7684-2431-3

ISBN 13: 978-0-7684-2431-7

This book and all other Destiny Image, Revival Press, MercyPlace, Fresh Bread, Destiny Image Fiction, and Treasure House books are available at Christian bookstores and distributors worldwide.

For a U.S. bookstore nearest you, call
1-800-722-6774.

For more information on foreign distributors, call
717-532-3040.

Or reach us on the Internet:
www.destinyimage.com

1 2 3 4 5 6 7 8 9 10 11 / 09 08 07

CONTENTS

PART 1

A LAUGHING MATTER

CHAPTER 1

WHY LAUGH?

It's fun to laugh!

Those four words, when it comes right down to it, would be a good enough answer to the question, "Why laugh?" for most people I know.

Think of playing with a little baby who is gradually getting in touch with the world around her (assuming it is a girl as my three babies were). When you talk to her, more often than not you smile. After a few weeks she begins to smile back. Before too long, one day you pick her up, lift her into the air, quickly bring her back down again, and her smile turns into a laugh. When this happens, you immediately lift her up again and she laughs again. This time you laugh with her. Now you're *both* having fun!

After that, if you're like me, you make her laugh just about every time you're near her. Soon she begins to hold out her arms, coaxing you to pick her up and make her laugh again. What's going on? You're communicating with your child! Long before she starts to learn how to say words, you are having fun together. Laughing is fun!

Suppose you're in a restaurant eating alone as I frequently do because I travel so much. Since you don't have anyone to talk to, you pass the time of day looking around at the other customers in the restaurant. As soon as you begin to do this, you can't help but notice that the people at certain tables seem to be having more fun than those at other tables. How can you tell they are having fun? They're laughing!

Laughter, like music, is a universal language. Hand gestures and bodily mannerisms often are culture-specific or indigenous to a particular nation or region, but smiling and laughter are the same the world over. A warm smile or a friendly laugh transcends any language barrier. Even people who don't speak the same language can have fun when they laugh together.

A Teacher, Not a Humorist

I have written this book, *Let's Laugh!*, because I love to make people laugh, and I do it all the time. I also want to help you build your confidence in your ability to make people laugh and show you how to do it. Making people laugh is not as hard as you might think. It is mainly a matter of knowing your audience, learning what kind of humor works best for you and understanding the role humor plays in whatever you are trying to accomplish.

For example, I'm not a humorist or a comedian by any stretch of the imagination. I'm a teacher. I teach people both in the classroom as well as in larger public gatherings. Now, here's the difference between a humorist who makes people laugh and a teacher who makes people laugh. For a humorist, laughing is an end in itself. If you can get people to laugh, you have accomplished your purpose. You're a good humorist or comedian, whichever term you prefer.

It is different for the teacher. Humor for a teacher is not an end in itself, but a means to an end. And by the way, the end for a skilled teacher is not even teaching; it is learning. Suppose a brilliant teacher teaches good material in a logical and convincing manner, but nobody learns anything. Has that teacher been successful? Of course not. No matter how much you teach, if your students don't learn, you are not a good teacher. Period!

Even though it took me quite a bit of time to figure it out, I eventually discovered that students in the classroom or in the auditorium will learn more if they are having fun than if they are gloomy, bored, sleepy, or just trying to take notes the best they can in order to pass the final exam. Consequently, I use humor all the time. If humor helps my students have fun and learn more, then humor also helps me to be a successful teacher. I don't want to be a good comedian; I want to be a good teacher.

My reason for telling you all these things about myself is to help you understand the approach I personally take toward humor and laughter. Over the years I have built up quite a good library on humor, and as I have read the books I have discovered that different authors tend to take different approaches to the subject. Some of these books have helped me to improve my humor. But others have not, simply because I do not find myself resonating well with some of them. This is not a matter of right or wrong; it is simply a matter of fit.

Humorless Books on Humor

Surprisingly enough, some authors write entire books on humor that are, for all intents and purposes, humorless. They write on the theory of humor. They analyze humor in the writings of Aristotle or Napoleon, Jesus or Churchill, or some other famous person, and they manage to do it in a boring way! Some write textbooks on humor apparently designed to do nothing more than help a student memorize enough material to pass a college course. Some of these books even include a whole section of jokes which, for some reason, I didn't think were very funny when I read them. The authors were not walking on the same road that I was. My main point here is that I believe that it is good for readers of books on humor to know where the author is coming from in order to get a feel for the jokes he or she includes in the book. It is helpful also as you read to keep in mind both the setting and the type of audience you expect to encounter most often. This will help you evaluate the appropriateness of the jokes you find in various sources.

I told you earlier that I am a teacher, but I didn't say what kind. Actually, I'm a Christian minister, so I do almost all my teaching in religious settings. For one thing, my students are almost always adults rather than children or youth.

Typically, the students in my classes have a median age of around the mid-forties. The same is true in the conferences of several hundred that I do from time to time. Occasionally, I even speak to congregations from the pulpit in a typical church setting.

No matter where I am teaching, I naturally have certain things that I want my hearers to learn. And since I want to make my sermon or my lesson or my speech fun, I use humor. Almost without exception I have found that, regardless of the setting or the size of the audience, whenever I use humor effectively my students learn more than if I had been dead serious and never given them reason or opportunity to laugh.

The humor I have concentrated on through many years is the kind that will make religiously-informed people in groups of anywhere from twenty to two thousand laugh. And that is the approach to humor that I am taking in this book. And by the way, you will not find any jokes in this book (except those in the section, "Jokes You're Not Supposed to Tell") that I have used on more than one occasion to make people laugh. They actually work quite well in the kinds of situations I have told you about. Whenever I include exceptions to that rule, for one reason or another, I will tell you.

Many of the jokes included in this book will probably work for you. Try them out!

What Laughing Does

I know from much experience that making my students laugh has tremendously beneficial effects on the atmosphere of the classroom or the auditorium or the church sanctuary. But I'm also a curious person. What's going on? What's so special about laughter? Why do students learn better and learn more in an environment of laughter and humor than in one where silence or seriousness is the order of the day? Does humor in a classroom setting do more than simply alleviate boredom?

Fortunately, I'm not the first one who has asked these questions. Many others before me have sought the answers. As a result, we have today a good bit of common knowledge about the dynamics that occur in humorous environments.

From the teacher's point of view, humor produces two major effects among students in a learning environment. One is a social effect and the other is a physical effect.

"I Like My Teacher!"

Regarding the social effect, humor helps an audience or a classroom of students relax with the speaker/teacher as well as with each other, even when they have never met before. Effective public speakers are aware of the value of the "ice breaker" in setting their audience at ease. The ice breaker is especially useful and necessary when the teacher and the students are together for the first time. After all, they are complete strangers. The unspoken question in the back of every student's mind as the teacher first takes his or her place in front of them is, "Am I going to like this person?" They experience a certain amount of tension as they try to anticipate whether the next hour or the next ten or twenty hours (if it is a whole course) will be a pleasant experience or just something they must endure in order to gather some needed information, pass an examination or earn a course credit.

A good ice breaker will implant in students' minds the idea that what is going to happen will be fun. Part of this is the anticipation that the ice breaker itself is probably just the beginning of more humor to come. A good teacher will not disappoint his or her students in this regard. Having said this, however, let me hasten to add the reminder that at the end of the day the value of the experience for the students will not be in how much they *laughed* but in how much they *learned*. Make no mistake about it; laughter and learning are closely related. Humor makes learning fun. Don't you learn more from a teacher you like and who makes you laugh than from a teacher who is serious and "all business" all the time?

When I am meeting my students on the first day of an entire course, I use as an ice breaker the suggestion that, since we will be together for several hours, they will understand more about what I am teaching if they know a bit about who I am. So I proceed to tell them a few stories from some of the life experiences of me and my family. Over the years, I have discovered that certain stories typically produce the most laughs, so I use them over and over again. They continue to work as ice breakers even when some of my students have heard them before. Often, those who already know what is coming nod their heads as a signal to me, broad smiles on their faces as they anticipate, along with me, the moment when the rest of the class will break out laughing. They laugh, too. We all have fun! We like each other!

No matter how much or how little time you have to teach, there is always room for a little humor. In fact, I believe that humor is important enough to *make room* for it in any presentation. It doesn't have to be long. Sometimes, in my case, time constraints or the size of the audience prohibit the use of my regular stories. In such situations I use a joke as an ice breaker. A canned joke! I am aware that some experts on humor advise against telling canned jokes, but they can't convince me. My jokes work. Later on I'll give you some of the reasons why I think they do.

Neutralizing Hostility

Another positive social effect of humor is its ability to neutralize potential hostility. I find this particularly useful when speaking or teaching about a controversial subject, as I frequently do. Every successful debater knows that dropping a good one-liner at the right time can be very effective in persuading an audience. Is there risk involved? Of course. The wrong kind of humor can backfire, build walls, and produce negative attitudes. One of my purposes is to help you avoid such situations. I have developed a certain expertise in this because of the many times that my own humor has backfired and caused people in my audience to dislike me rather than like me. Experience is a wonderful teacher. The only way to learn to use humor is by using it and then drawing lessons from your experiences—both successes and failures.

Humor, when skillfully applied, will assure you that your audience is understanding what you are trying to teach. This is especially true when your humor has a direct application to the point you happen to be making at the time. By saying this, I do not mean to imply that every joke or humorous line you use has to relate directly to the subject at hand. But each one will be good to the degree that it makes people laugh.

Someone has said that laughter has always been an inexpensive, non-fattening, contagious, and pleasant way to relieve tension and hostility.

People laughing at your humor is a sure sign that you have their attention. Laughter is valuable instant feedback from your audience to you. Use humor freely but not excessively. Unless you are a comedian, you should not be trying to elicit constant laughter. But your audience will pay more attention to your serious content if you do give them an opportunity to laugh from time to time. My rule of thumb is that if I teach for an hour, I am disappointed in my presentation if my listeners don't laugh, say, half a dozen times.

I know of studies that reveal clear relationships between humor, paying attention and consequent retention of the material presented. For a teacher, this is the bottom line. Some of you who are reading this may be saying to yourself right about now, "I don't have enough of a sense of humor to pull something like this off." I understand how you feel because I once felt the same way. Later on I will show you how easy it really is to make people laugh and thereby improve your communication with others.

Humor is especially useful if your audience contains many people who do not know each other. Being surrounded by strangers can cause you to erect a psychological wall between you and the speaker. This wall drops very quickly when you and everyone else around you is laughing. You might even find yourself looking at a complete stranger next to you and agreeing with that person that the joke is funny. Humor has a very subtle way of getting us to lower our defenses, set aside our skepticism and open our minds to receive what is being presented.

Laughing will actually make your audience look better to you. People are prettier smiling than when they have a dazed, bored, neutral, angry, disapproving or, especially, a sour look on their faces. Not only does humor make the audience like you more but it also helps you like your audience more. This kind of positive rapport and connection with your audience sharpens your thinking and helps you be more relaxed in your presentation. A healthy mood of humor is much easier to sustain throughout once it is established at the beginning with a good ice breaker. One good laugh will set the stage for another. Sustained, easy laughter is a dependable indicator that the people are receptive to whatever else you are saying. If they are laughing, they are not whining or complaining or turning you off. Laughter establishes a strong bonding between speaker and listeners.

Laughing Makes You Healthy!

Aside from its positive social effects, humor also provides genuine health benefits. Simply stated, people who laugh are healthier than people who do not. The Bible hinted at this thousands of years ago when it said, *"A merry heart does good, like medicine"* (Prov. 17:22a).

Those were pre-scientific days. But modern science has since confirmed that the Bible, as always, was right. The scientists who study this are called—get ready for this one because it has no fewer than nine syllables—psychoneuroimmunologists. They are beginning to map out the different ways that various mental attitudes and thought processes can affect the physical body. One of these is laughter, which is especially effective as a stress reliever. In these days when stress levels in our whirlwind society are higher than ever before, laughter becomes even more important. And, as a medicine, it is notably cost effective. Laughter costs nothing. Everybody can afford it and it always delivers great returns for even a small investment.

Laughter energizes and exercises the body in a way similar to aerobic conditioning. And it seems as though our bodies are designed for smiling and laughter. For example, it requires fewer muscles to smile than to frown. A healthy dose of laughter can lift our spirits and help us see the world in a more positive light.

Not too many people thought much about the physical benefits of laughter until a celebrity, Norman Cousins of the *Saturday Review*, told his personal story some years ago in a book titled *Anatomy of an Illness*. It seems that Cousins had been suffering from a potentially crippling disease, a rare affliction of the bones and connective tissue called ankylosing splonylitus. One of the symptoms was chronic, severe pain. On some of his most difficult days, he discovered that a good belly laugh tended to reduce the pain. He knew that stress could cause illness, and he began to realize that laughing could be an antidote. Through experimentation he found that ten minutes of sustained laughter made it possible for him to sleep pain-free for two or more hours at a time!

Cousins' therapy included watching humorous videos like the Marx Brothers or *Candid Camera*. Sure enough, a steady diet of humor helped him recover, and his story was publicized through the media and even through medical journals.

What's Going On?

What happens in the body when we laugh? A lot of things. For a starter, a large number of muscles, otherwise mostly unused, begin to contract. Stomach muscles, chest muscles, and shoulder muscles all get a workout. With really hard laughter, muscles in the face, the arms and the legs join in. In fact, fifteen small muscles in the face go into action, which increases blood flow and gives us a kind of pleasant glow on our faces. Some have estimated that twenty seconds of a good laugh provides the exercise equivalent of ten minutes on a rowing machine! Laughing is a lot like "inner jogging."

When you laugh your heart rate increases and your blood pressure goes up. However, when you finish, they quickly return to normal, which means that you have just successfully processed some stress. All this activates your diaphragm, which pumps your lungs and gives you a good infusion of oxygen, thereby enriching your blood. At the same time, your endothelium—the tissue of the lining of your blood vessels—expands and increases the flow of this enriched blood, just as it does when you are on a treadmill. You find yourself with more energy and creativity!

Contrast this with the effect on the body of a melancholy spirit. Sadness, boredom and depression all drain the body of energy, excitement and enthusiasm. Lethargy and apathy set in. This is one reason why depressed people seem to be tired all the time and want to do little other than sleep.

As time goes by, curious medical researchers uncover more and more physical benefits of humor. One group found that humor stimulates the brain to release dopamine, a chemical messenger that induces a euphoric feeling of peace and calmness similar to that which comes with eating chocolate or having sex. The downside is that dopamine can become addictive and cause certain individuals to overindulge in laughter, turning them into those we would call "silly people." There are some indications that laughing can help control glucose levels in diabetics. It may even activate the immune system by releasing immunoglobulins.

This field of study has advanced to the point where there is now an American Association of Therapeutic Humor, whose website is found at www.aath.org. Some specialists in this field like to be called "mirthologists!" That might make a good *Jeopardy* question!

Healthy Grief

Humor also plays a significant role in our ability to process grief in a healthy manner. Some individuals seem to handle grief much better than others. Losing a loved one is a good example. I think that everyone would agree that proper mourning is necessary for good mental health, but some people carry their mourning to a pathological extreme. Years later they are still grieving. Black bunting and pictures of the deceased still adorn the walls of their home. The deceased's clothing still hangs in the closet, shoes still rest on the floor and personal items still lie on the dresser. Everything remains untouched, as if the deceased merely stepped out for a few moments. In the minds of the mourners, any kind of joy, humor or laughter would be a sign of disrespect for the memory of their loved one.

Those who recover from a tragedy most rapidly and most completely are those who quickly learn to see the bright side. They look for the silver lining in the dark cloud. Laughter to them is not disrespectful, but healing. Their reasoning? If their loved one were here, he or she would want the survivor to be happy, not sad. Being ready and willing to laugh can help turn sorrow into joy and hasten the healing process.

I think of a recently widowed friend of mine. Although she deeply loved her husband of thirty years, she refused to go into the tunnel of a pity party after he died. Her sense of humor carried her into the next phase of her life in a very positive manner. As an example, she once set off the buzzer in the security line in an airport. The agents took her aside and patted her down. When they finished, she thanked them and said, "By the way, would you mind doing that again? I lost my husband two years ago, and that felt pretty good!" Even the security agents laughed with her! Humor heals!

Where Are We Going?

Where are we going with this science of "mirthology"? Who knows? Laughter may not become a cure-all for anything that ever ails us, but it certainly can't hurt! Laughter is free, painless (unless your sides are splitting!) and carries no possible negative side effects. It has no calories, is not fattening and contains no toxic chemicals or artificial sweeteners. And not only is laughter not harmful, it is positively healthful!

What do strangers do when they first meet each other? Whether it's on an elevator or in an airplane, in the church lobby after a service, in a waiting room or at a cocktail party, they attempt to make each other smile. Better yet, they try to stimulate a laugh, or at least a chuckle. Why do they do this? Laughter creates rapport. It helps everyone involved to relax and quickly take a liking to each other. Laughter initiates a positive relationship.

Laughter not only helps us physically, but it also helps us socially. It can help us overcome embarrassment. It can build bridges. It can heal differences. Laughter makes life more pleasant for everybody. It's much better to laugh than not to laugh!

So?

So, let's laugh!

CHAPTER 2

WHO SHOULD LAUGH?

Based on what I have said so far, everybody should laugh. Don't you agree? A good laugh is good medicine for anybody. It always tastes sweet going down and never has a bitter aftertaste! Our bodies are built for laughter. We are tailor-made to enjoy life and to find levity often in our daily circumstances. People who only laugh a little bit or who don't laugh at all are clearly missing out on their full destiny. Some people are so serious and uptight about life that they never can relax and enjoy living. And they make everyone around them uptight as well. If you have ever met someone who seemed to have no sense of humor you probably know what I mean. There's something wrong with them!

I say this because I believe that God's design for human beings and human society includes humor. Laughter is instinctual; even newborn babies respond naturally to a warm smile and gentle laughter. And at only a few months of age they are laughing themselves!

Laughter is also transcultural. People in different cultures may laugh at different things, but they do laugh. It's part of normal life. I travel internationally quite a bit and often find myself in a country whose language I do not understand. But when I'm in public places such as an airport or a restaurant, a shopping mall or anyplace where people are socializing, I don't need to understand the language to tell who is having a good time and who is not. Those who are smiling and laughing are having a better time than those who are scowling.

Think about it. Humans are the only beings in all creation that laugh and weep with a solid knowledge of why. We humans can weep over the realization that we weep and laugh over the realization that we laugh. If we want to, we can even analyze why we do either one, although, as I mentioned in the last chapter, analyzing why we laugh frequently turns out to be a boring exercise. In practice, though, people experiencing real fear or pain seem nevertheless to have a built-in ability to counteract whatever misery they find themselves in by an intuitive use of humor. It can range from a smile to a belly laugh.

No matter where you go around the world, you will find that a smile is an instant, mutually understood form of communication. Even if while shopping you have to point and use sign language, the smile on the face of the sales clerk, and your smile in return, will cover most of the bases. Smiling is as much a human trait as chewing or walking. You don't have to learn how; you just have to learn how to do it well at the right time and in the right place.

Will Everyone Laugh?

O.K., let's admit that everyone *should* laugh. Here is the next question we could ask: *Will* everyone laugh? The answer is yes and no.

If I am with a group of four or five around a lunch table, for example, and the subject of humor comes up, I can usually pull up a joke that I'm sure will make every one around the table laugh. At the same time I know down deep that some of the laughs might well be "courtesy laughs," especially if I'm paying for the lunch, which is frequently the case.

Speaking of courtesy laughs, let me bring up an important point: What do you do if someone starts telling you a joke that you have heard before? I think I have some good advice, especially if you want to improve in your ability to use humor. Since I tell a lot of jokes when I am emceeing a conference, individual conferees routinely corner me during a break, look at me with a twinkle in their eye, and say, "Peter, I've got a joke for you." Even if I'm in a hurry, I try to stop, return their eye twinkle, and say, "Let's hear it!"

By the way, I have learned not to say something like, "O.K., I need a good joke for a change because mine are so bad!" True, this line is self-deprecating, which is not a bad way to be from time to time. But this is not the way to do it. Why? Simply because you should never tell a bad joke, at least not more than once or twice. If your jokes are really going to make people laugh, you are the first one who needs to believe that all your jokes are good. It is an application of the power of positive thinking, like a batter believing he can hit the ball. If you train yourself to think this way, your jokes will make more people laugh and they will laugh harder.

Have You Heard This One?

Back to the, "I've got a joke for you." When the person begins telling the joke, I listen attentively and try to show it by my body language. Very frequently, after a line or two, he or she will pause and say, "Have you heard this one before?" At this point I have to be truthful. If I haven't heard it or if at the time I don't think I've heard it, I say, "No, go on." But suppose I have heard it? The last thing I want to do is to say words to the effect, "Oh, yeah, I've heard that one!" Why? Because it amounts to a put down. It can leave the subtle implication that I feel superior to my friend and am already way ahead of him or her where humor is concerned.

Saying "Yes, I've heard that one," also amounts to a let down. He or she really wanted to tell me the joke. It took a certain amount of courage and planning on his or her part to catch me and talk to me. It also takes courage to share with someone else a joke you think is funny. What if the other person doesn't think it is funny? The individual sharing the joke with me really thinks it is funny; otherwise, why tell it at all? And why should I deprive that person of the pleasure of returning a favor and sharing a joke with me?

So, what do I say? I don't say whether I've heard it or not. Instead, I say, "Go ahead, I want to hear it." That's usually all the encouragement the person needs. But I have an ulterior motive behind all of this. I may have heard the joke before; indeed, I may even have told it many times myself, but there is always room for improvement. Suppose he or she tells the joke better than I ever have. Maybe there is a new twist or a funnier way to deliver the punch line. Perhaps it has a better build up. Who knows? In any case, I am the winner. If I haven't heard it before, I may have a great new joke to add to my repertoire. And if I have heard it, I enjoy the pleasure of hearing it again and from a different perspective. Even more important, the person who told me the joke wins also. We both enjoy a good laugh and he or she goes away affirmed and with greater confidence about sharing humor.

That is why, no matter whether I've heard the joke before or not, I always laugh hard when the joke is over. The laugh makes me feel good for the reasons I mentioned in the last chapter. It makes my friend feel good because the "amateur" has matched the "professional," so to speak. Then, if I have actually heard the joke before, I usually say, "Yeah, I've heard it, but I never heard it told like that! Thank you!" We're both happy. If my friend thinks that I meant he or she told it *better* than I've ever heard it before, that's o.k. with me. In the best of all worlds, humor is fun for both the teller and the listener.

Put-Downs

Let's talk some more about put-downs. We've all heard it said that beauty is in the eye of the beholder. In the same way, humor is in the ear of the listener. While everyone *should* laugh, one good reason why some people *won't* laugh at a certain joke is because they feel that the joke degrades a certain kind of individual or group of individuals. Put-down jokes are mean. Nothing will upset or alienate an audience more than their perception that you are poking fun at them, at someone in their group or at someone close to them, particularly if you appear to be violating the political correctness of the day. Notice the word "perception." In your mind the joke may be harmless, gentle, and by no stretch of the imagination a put-down. You might even be able to argue that point persuasively. But none of that matters if the listener perceives it to be something else.

For example, I once heard an ice-breaker joke that was well-meaning but that turned out to be a subtle put-down. After a rather elaborate introduction, the speaker went to the platform and said:

"Thank you for those very gracious words of introduction. I could have listened to something like that all morning! And for a while there I thought I was going to have to!"

The remark certainly drew a big laugh from the audience. But what else did it do? It also put down the introducer. The speaker could have taken the edge off of the put-down by, for example, making eye contact with the introducer, good-naturedly pointing a finger, and saying it as if just the two of them were privy to the attempted joke. But here is a similar ice-breaker that avoids the put-down altogether:

"Thank you very much for the introduction. It made me feel like the bug that hit the windshield. I didn't know I had it in me!"

For years one of my best jokes had to do with the School of Psychology in Fuller Theological Seminary, where I was teaching. I thought it was a good joke because even the faculty members of the School of Psychology laughed when I told it. It had multiple punch lines that always worked. But one day, however, I had a rude awakening. After telling the joke that day a member of the audience who was a mental health worker came up to me during the break. She very tactfully and politely suggested to me that my joke could be perceived as poking fun at people who suffered from the mental illnesses that were mentioned in the joke. Realizing instantly that she was right, I thanked her and told her that I would not tell the joke any more—and I haven't. That is why I haven't even included it in the section later on called, "Jokes You Shouldn't Tell."

There are some fine lines here. If you are unmistakably a member of the group being made fun of, you are less at risk of being perceived as using a put down because you are poking fun at yourself. Making fun of yourself is generally acceptable. For example, at the time of this writing I am 75 years old and no one could doubt that I qualify as a senior citizen. Later on I have a whole section on senior citizen jokes. Even though so-called "ageism" is frowned upon by our society these days, I can get away with telling jokes on us senior citizens. In fact, some of my best jokes are senior citizen jokes.

On the other hand, I don't know exactly where to draw the line with "aggie" jokes. The general thrust of these jokes revolves around the stereotype that "aggies" are dumb. As it turns out, "aggie" jokes are really funny. I told "aggie" jokes for quite a while, always prefaced by the explanation that I myself am an "aggie". I am a farmer by background and my Bachelor of Science degree is from Rutgers University College of Agriculture. Students in the College of Arts and Sciences habitually referred to us, derogatorily, as "aggies," so I qualify as a member of the group being put down.

I had a lot of fun with those jokes until the day I found myself in a rural area talking to an audience of farmers. I used my normal routine, but since they knew that currently I wasn't a *practicing* farmer, they were not convinced that I was really one of the group I was joking about. In their perception I was an outsider poking fun at their group. Needless to say, that was not one of my most notable days for using humor.

In fact, I have hardly, if ever, used "aggie" jokes since, even for audiences that I could easily convince that I was an "aggie" and therefore "permitted" to poke fun at them. I still think "aggie" jokes are pretty good jokes, but I am no longer certain that they are appropriate.

Ethnic Jokes

Ethnic jokes are some of the riskiest jokes to tell. Even when told with good-natured intentions, ethnic jokes told in the wrong setting or by the wrong person can result in misunderstanding, offense, insult and resentment. They can also inadvertently reinforce latent prejudice and bigotry.

Since I am a white, Anglo-Saxon American male, I clearly could not pretend to be a member of any ethnic minority. So I avoid ethnic jokes, except for the Hittite joke and maybe one or two other safe ones that I will tell later on. One of my best friends, however, who is a Korean-American, does qualify to tell certain ethnic jokes. Here is one of his better ice-breakers:

"As you can see, I'm Asian. I know that a lot of you Americans can't tell one Asian man from another. If you've seen one, you've seen them all. You might have an especially hard time telling the difference between Chinese and Japanese and Koreans, so I'll tell you how it's done. If the Asian looks really smart, he's probably Chinese. If he looks rich, he's probably Japanese. But if he looks handsome, he's Korean!"

This always gets a good laugh, even from Chinese and Japanese. It puts no one down, it highlights true characteristics that Chinese and Japanese are proud of and it actually puts down the Koreans, my friend included, because everyone who hears the joke knows the punch line is nothing but an incongruous spoof, reflecting wishful thinking. Not only does the audience laugh, but from then on, they decide that they like my friend. Consequently, he's ready to roll as soon as he tells the joke!

I also have a Chinese-American friend who does a take off on the same ice breaker. After the first part of the joke, he gives this variation:

"If the Asian is handsome, he will be the Korean. If he looks rich, he will be the Japanese. But if he is handsome, rich, and intelligent, he is the Chinese!"

Keep in mind, however, that even though my friends are bona fide members of American ethnic minorities, they would never tell a joke, for example, on African-Americans. In US urban areas, Asians and African-Americans are not always on the best of terms, so anything from an Asian that could be taken as an insult to African-Americans would be seen as ill-natured. Funny as it might be, the joke would not stimulate rapport; it would more likely precipitate hostility.

The same holds true for Caucasians telling jokes on African-Americans or African-Americans telling jokes on Caucasians or anyone telling jokes about someone outside their particular ethnic grouping. The risk of generating mis-understanding, enmity or hostility are too great. For this reason, ethnic jokes are better avoided.

Group Dynamics

If you tell jokes like I do, as a speaker to an audience, it is important that you understand group dynamics. As a rule of thumb, the larger the group, the more likely you will get a good laugh. Why? Because laughter is contagious. Laughter spawns laughter. People laugh when they see and hear other people laugh. This is why television producers pump canned recordings of laughter into their sitcoms. People at home imagine that a large crowd is watching a live production, laughing hard at each punch line, and they tend to join in with them, matching laugh for laugh. I am contin-ually surprised at the number of passengers on an airplane who actually laugh out loud at sitcom videos. The people around them on the plane usually are not laughing, but the sound track gives the viewers the feeling that they are.

Despite the contagious nature of laughter, however, you can depend on the fact that not everyone in an audience will laugh hard when you tell a joke. Some may not laugh at all—at first. This is to be expected because some people have more of a sense of humor than others. There usually will be at least a few sitting out there with somber or deadpan faces, as if daring you to make them laugh. You may even run into a few who resist even your best efforts and never even crack a smile, much less laugh out loud. But those types of folks will be rare. In general, everything will tend to balance out. When real live people sitting near the more serious listeners are laughing, some of the more reluctant ones will begin to lose their inhibitions and laugh along as well. That's the way group dynamics works.

When the majority of my audience is women, I know ahead of time that my jokes will be better. I remember reading somewhere that some researchers once found that men go more for one-liners and slapstick humor like *The Three Stooges*, while women respond best to a story with a punch line—the kind of jokes I use most often. In other words, men tend to respond more to visual humor while women respond to verbal humor. The reason is simple: women tend to analyze humor more than men do, and as a result derive more pleasure from the joke's punch line.

In a classroom, where the audience is smaller, the critical mass for this phenomenon of group dynamics to operate is seventeen. It is difficult to use and sustain group humor with less than seventeen. Twelve or fewer are virtually hopeless, and I don't even attempt to use jokes with that size group.

Laughing In Church

I mentioned in chapter one that I am a Christian minister. Almost all of my audiences, large or small, are made up of Christian believers who take their faith very seriously. This can be a real challenge to someone who likes to tell jokes and make people laugh.

Attitudes toward humor among Christians will vary, usually according to the congregation or denomination they belong to. At one time I tried to classify denominations according to a make believe "humor quotient." Presbyterians, for some reason, came in at the bottom. Whenever I tell a joke to Presbyterians I seem to get, at the best, a polite groan from the audience. On the other hand, most Episcopalians love humor. When I mentioned this to one Episcopal priest, he said to me, "Do you want to know why?" After I told him that I did, he said, "Wherever you find four Episcopalians together, you'll always find a fifth!" Apparently, they enjoy special help!

Baptists usually have an above average humor quotient; they love a good joke, even (or especially) in church. Mennonites tend to be sour. Lutherans are in between. Assemblies of God, like their Baptist brethren, love good humor. Many Assemblies of God pastors customarily start each sermon with a joke. As best I can recall, I have lost control of an audience only once because of sidesplitting laughter, and that was with a group of Assemblies of God pastors from a largely rural district in North Carolina. It happened back in the days when I was still telling my "aggie" jokes. The pastors weren't farmers but their churches were full of them. It took them a long, long time to stop laughing at my series of "aggie" jokes and get serious about the real topic we had come together to study.

That took place in North Carolina, which reminds me of another rule of thumb: People from the south tend to have a better sense of humor than people from the north. For example, one of the hardest places to tell jokes is in New England. I don't know why this particular dynamic works as it does. It probably has something to do with the local or regional culture as well as the ethnic, social, political, religious and economic background and heritage of the people.

Furthermore, when we begin comparing, for example, Presbyterians (low humor quotient) to Assemblies of God (high humor quotient), a socio-economic factor enters the picture. Presbyterians in general have one of the highest levels of family income of all American denominations. Assemblies of God congregations, on the other hand, typically consist mainly of lower middle class to lower class people. The general rule of thumb is that blue-collar people tend to appreciate straight out jokes more than do upper-class, college educated people, like Presbyterians, who tend to prefer more "sophisticated" humor.

Even so, I have found that although Presbyterians tend to groan at the first joke or two, if I am with them for a while and if I persist with my jokes, they will in most cases overcome their cultural inhibitions and begin laughing out loud, and sometimes even laughing hard, before I am finished. Depending on the group, making people laugh is not always easy but it *can* be done!

Why are some Christians reluctant to laugh in church? It is true that Jesus said, *"Every idle word that men shall speak, they shall give account thereof in the day of judgment"* (Matthew 12:36 KJV). But anyone who equates an "idle word" with humor has, in my opinion, a twisted view of the Christian life. One of the fruits of the Holy Spirit is joy! Christians full of joy are therefore more spiritual and closer to fulfilling their purpose and destiny than are those who somehow equate gloominess with godliness. Such people must be idealizing the medieval monasteries, which were extremely serious religious centers. No wonder: the monks who lived in monasteries had to take vows of poverty, chastity and obedience! Some even took a vow of silence. If I lived there, I promise you, I would be gloomy also!

And what about religious jokes? Some claim that religious jokes are sacrilegious. It all depends on whether you are making fun *of* Christianity or if you are making fun *with* Christianity. Since I am a Christian minister, I have a license to make fun *with* Christianity, and I do it all the time. I can't do the same with jokes about Islam, Judaism, Hinduism or any other religion. There may be exceptions, such as the joke about what you get when you cross a Jehovah's Witness with a Unitarian: You get someone who goes door to door without knowing why! But that's the exception, not the rule.

When we get to the jokes in Part Two, I have a whole section on religious jokes. I believe that the more we laugh in church the better!

CHAPTER 3

WHAT MAKES THEM LAUGH?

I recently read that in England a group of scientists have developed a mathematical formula for rating jokes. According to these eminent intellectuals, the "humor quotient" of a given joke can be determined by using the equation: $x = (fl + n°) / p$. Please don't ask me how to use this formula because it's way over my head. However, it supposedly is designed to rate a joke from a low of 0 to a high of 200. (Can you believe it? Somebody actually spent valuable *research dollars* developing this!) By the way, just what *is* a "humor quotient" anyway? How can something as intangible and unpredictable as humor possibly be measured by anything remotely approaching mathematical precision?

Predictably, this scientific approach to humor has provoked widespread ridicule, especially among professional comedians. They know through practice and experience that many different variables are involved in making people laugh and that none of them can be programmed into a formula. Sometimes, for instance, the voice, the body language, the facial expression and the demeanor of the joke teller are as funny or even funnier than the joke itself. In live or face-to-face comedy, as in every other form of verbal communication, the visual aspect is absolutely critical to success. This factor alone is enough to call into question the validity of this "scientific" equation and its so-called "humor quotient."

These British scientists have one idea about what makes people laugh. But others, particularly those who are personally involved in humor, have their own, better ideas derived from their experiences "in the trenches." Nothing can take the place of personal experience. Humor is an elusive quantity so subjective that I personally do not believe it can be reduced to a mathematical formula. Like others who deal regularly with humor, I have my own personal ideas about what makes people laugh. But I would also be quick to say that I would not expect everyone else who wants to make people laugh to do it the way I do. I know my audiences and I have learned through experience what I can get away with. I also know what bombs for me. A joke that I can tell successfully might not work for someone else and vice versa.

The World's Funniest Joke

For example, a poll conducted by a team of psychologists in England revealed what they rated as "the world's funniest joke." Here it is:

> Sherlock Holmes and Dr. Watson are going camping. They pitch their tent under the stars and go to sleep.

Sometime in the middle of the night, Holmes wakes Watson up and says, "Watson, look up at the stars and tell me what you deduce."

Watson answers, I see millions of stars and if even a few of those have planets, it's quite likely there are some planets like Earth, and if there are a few planets like Earth out there, there might also be life."

Holmes replies, "Watson, you idiot, somebody stole our tent!"

———

This joke, I will admit, is funny. I, however, would never use it. If I tried this joke on one of my audiences, I could anticipate nothing more than a polite chuckle in response. On a scale of one to ten I would rate it, perhaps, as a six. Why? First of all, this joke depends for its effect on what is known as "derision theory." Holmes puts one over on Watson. By referring to Watson as an "idiot," Holmes puts Watson in his place, thereby showing himself to be superior to the good doctor. The listener is supposed to think, "I'm glad I'm not as dumb as Watson," and externalize that feeling of relief through laughter. This joke may fit the British sense of humor well, but not so much the American.

Secondly, this particular joke has its greatest potential for laughs with audiences who have more than a passing acquaintance with the personalities and the stereotypical roles of Sherlock Holmes and Dr. Watson. Most of the people who make up my middle-American audiences probably would recognize the names but many of them would know little more than that. This joke might be rated the funniest joke in England, where Sherlock Holmes is a household name, but probably would be received differently in other parts of the world. I have at least fifty jokes in my personal collection that I think are funnier than this one. But that is only my personal opinion, of course. You might be able to tell the Holmes and Watson joke and get a great response. Remember, humor is in the ear of the hearer. And its success depends on the skill and personality of the joke teller.

Long build-Up, Hilarious Punch Line

One conclusion drawn from the application of the humor equation $x = (fl + n°) / p$, according to those who understand it, is that the best jokes have a long build-up followed by a hilarious punch line. In this instance I fully agree. That kind of joke is the chief ingredient in the laugh-producing package that I customarily use. This rule, for obvious reasons of course, applies only to jokes, not to one-liners or other humorous side remarks.

In my reading of literature on the theory of humor—and I have read quite a bit of it—I have been surprised at the number of authors who advise against using jokes. Naturally, this caught my attention because a huge percentage of the humor that I use happens to be jokes. The author of one article I read avowed that the joke died back around 1975. The article was accompanied by a cartoon which had an R.I.P. tombstone on the grave of the joke. I was puzzled until I read a bit further and discovered that this conclusion was based on the findings of professional comedians. Then it made sense to me.

As I have said already, I am not a professional comedian; I am a teacher. Professional comics may have to depend on things like observational humor and one-liners because for them laughter is an end in itself. As a teacher, laughter is not my ultimate goal; teaching is. But laughter is an important means to that end. And since my ultimate goal is teaching, I can use jokes, I do use jokes, and my jokes are alive and well. They help my teaching. My jokes help create a relaxed environment that makes it easier for students to learn.

I was further puzzled by a serious article written to encourage preachers to use humor, but which warned them not to use jokes. The author advised preachers to draw their humor from life experiences because jokes are supposedly high-risk humor. If the punch line falls flat, everybody knows it and it is a setback for the speaker, but if the audience fails to see the humor in a life situation, no one is the worse. In other words, if you try to use a life situation to inject humor into your preaching and nobody laughs, just pretend it was an *illustration* and *not* a joke!

Joel's Jokes

As I was reading and reflecting on that article the thought occurred to me that preachers are at a disadvantage because they speak to the same audience week after week. Consequently, they can't recycle their jokes the way I can because my audiences constantly change.

At the time of this writing the most popular preacher in the United States is Joel Osteen of Lakewood Church in Houston. He preaches to about 30,000 parishioners weekly, not counting his huge television audience. And, wonder of wonders, he begins each sermon with a joke. Every time he stands up to preach, without fail, he pulls out a sheet of paper and reads a joke, a different one each week. To be perfectly honest, I personally find some of his jokes to be only moderately funny, say a seven on a scale of one to ten, but the people in the audience are so conditioned to this routine that they laugh whether or not the joke is really very funny.

Keep in mind what I just said because this is an important point. Does it matter how funny the joke is? Not at all! The only thing that matters is that the people laugh, and that is what helps them prepare to listen to the sermon.

What makes them laugh? The members of Lakewood Church laugh because Joel Osteen wants them to laugh, and they know that by doing so they are encouraging their pastor. They also laugh because they want to laugh. Laughing makes them feel better than they would if they didn't laugh. Sometimes they even laugh because the joke is actually funny! In any case, everybody wins and the show goes on. The people come back the following week and bring their friends.

Let me now describe for you my own modus operandi. Through years of practice, experimentation and experience I have discovered what makes people in my audiences laugh. My method may or may not work for other public speakers but it works for me.

A Joke-teller Reputation

For a starter, over the years I have gained the reputation of being a joke-teller. Telling jokes is one of my public trademarks, just as "Hi-Oh, Silver!" is for the Lone Ranger. If any episode of "The Lone Ranger" did not include at least one "Hi-Oh, Silver," something was wrong. The viewers of the show expected it and were disappointed if they did not hear it. It is the same way with my speaking. My audiences have come to expect hearing jokes from me and won't let me get away with not telling them any (not that I would want to anyway!).

On more than one occasion, during my opening remarks, someone apparently thought I was preparing to move into the more serious part of my talk, and to make sure I didn't forget, shouted out from the audience: "Joke! Joke!" And here I hadn't even finished my preliminaries! Do something long enough and consistently enough and people will associate that action with you and will be surprised or disappointed when you don't follow through every time.

It never fails; that spontaneous call for a joke always produces laughter from some of those in the audience. Milking the advantage, I always make a point to laugh right along with them and then, with a big grin on my face, say, "Don't worry, it's coming! Give me a couple more minutes!" Believe it or not, by that time the whole crowd usually is laughing. When people come into a place ready to laugh and expecting to laugh, it doesn't take much to make them laugh. All it requires is a little "priming of the pump."

What this means is that if the audience is well-conditioned for humor it is not necessary to surprise them or attempt to blindside them. Part of the whole fun package for everybody is to be completely upfront with the coming joke. Everybody knows it's coming and excitement and anticipation build, just as before the initial kick off in a football game.

So, I usually go ahead and bait the people a bit. I start off by announcing with a straight face, "My topic today is_____, so please get out your pencil and paper and get ready to take notes." Then I say, "But I am not quite ready," even as I am reaching into my upper left shirt pocket. In most cases, there are enough people in the audience who have heard me speak previously and they almost always spontaneously precipitate a combination of applause and laughter because they now know that the joke is coming. Believe me, it's truly a bonus to have people laughing before you even begin the joke! This common reaction is due in large part to my reputation as a joke-teller. Don't expect this kind of response from an audience when you are just getting started with using humor. As it was with me, it will take you some time to build a reputation.

I am well aware that some humor "experts" warn against the use of what they call "canned" jokes. Nevertheless, just about all of my jokes are canned. Canned jokes may be obsolete or "old hat" to some and may not work well for others, but I love them. Before I go on the platform to speak I always leaf through my joke file. I have taken the pains to type the jokes I feel I should keep. Once saved in my computer, I can simply select the ones I want, reduce them to a size that I can fold once and fit into my shirt pocket and then print them out.

Know When to Hold 'Em and When to Fold 'Em

How do I know which jokes to save and file away for later use and which ones to discard? First of all, before I will add a joke to my repertoire it must tickle my own personal funny bone. It has to be funny to me personally. I'm not going to tell a joke that I don't think rates at least a nine or a ten. Next, I hold the new joke until I get with an audience that already has laughed at several of my jokes. When I sense that the timing is right, I take out the new joke and say, "I'm going to experiment with you. I'm going to tell you a joke for the first time, something I rarely do. When I finish, tell me if it's a 'keeper.' Okay?" Then I go ahead and tell the joke simply as part of a test. When I finish, I usually get at least a courtesy laugh. I have been doing this long enough now that often I can sense by the level of laughter and by the audience's body language and facial expressions whether or not my new joke is a winner. Nevertheless, I ask the group, "Is this one a keeper?"

If what I perceive to be a "critical mass" says, "No!" I scrap the joke. On the other hand, if it becomes a keeper, I test it at least once more to make sure. Joke-telling is always a gamble and, as Kenny Rogers' hit song says, it's important to "know when to hold 'em and know when to fold 'em!"

Priming the Audience

Over the years I have developed a helpful methodology to use when I am with a new audience and need to "prime" them for humor. I usually start off with a few ice-breaker questions such as, "Where are you from?" and "How far did you travel to get here?" Then I ask, "How many of you are attending one of my conferences for the very first time?" As hands are raised throughout the room I ask everybody to look around and notice all the "newbies". This ploy helps to relax everybody, particularly the first-timers, who are reassured to know that they are not the only ones. This also works to build a bond of fellowship among the audience.

Next, I scan the crowd and say, "Wow! Over 50 percent!" I then pause for an instant, look real happy and excited, and say, "This means that I can tell my jokes!" That line almost always gets a good laugh. One reason for this may be that because my conferences are religious conferences most of the people are probably expecting some kind of somber or "stick-to-the-facts" presentation. I know that many of them go for weeks or even months without hearing any jokes at all in their churches, so for them this is a welcome change. Their laugh is a sign of relief at their discovery that, whatever else my conference may or may not be, at least it will not be boring!

With the audience now more relaxed, I continue, saying, "I know that some of you have heard these jokes before, but that doesn't matter. Please laugh the second time around!" This line, too, generally produces laughter throughout the room. Then I follow up with, "I know you will because they get funnier every time I tell them!" laughing as I say it, and they laugh with me. From this point on, I don't have to apologize for telling a joke they might have heard. In fact, many of them who have heard the joke before are rooting for me to tell it once again because they now want their friends to hear it. Some even have told me that they have laughed as hard on hearing a joke for the third, fourth or fifth time as they did the first time. Don't forget, my objective is not to tell them a joke they haven't heard before—my objective is to make them laugh.

Here's another rule of thumb: I would rather tell a "ten" five times than to tell ten new "fives!"

I don't always follow the same routine, but here is one I use quite often. I say, "I have a computer, but I don't plug it into the Internet or email. My reason is that I have read that there is such as thing as a medical condition called 'Internet addiction disorder,'— 'IAD!' Here's what it does." I then pull out a paper that obviously is the medical report. By now, the audience is catching on that I am spoofing them. I then read out loud: "IAD has been defined as a psychological dependence on the Internet that leads to clinically significant distress and/or diminished productivity!' Who wants that?" By now they're laughing at *me*.

I go on to say, "You can still send me an email. My email address is _____. I have a staff of about twenty people whose computers are plugged into the Internet. They get the emails, filter out what they think I should get and then give them to my wife who filters them some more. So I *might* get yours. However, I have carefully instructed my staff to, above all, save me all the jokes!" The audience loves this. I say,

"You'd be surprised at how many jokes there are on the Internet. I throw most of them away, but I do keep some. Like this one!" Then I reach into my shirt pocket to pull out the joke, and they laugh just at the act of reaching. By now we're all having such a good time that just about any joke will go over well.

My favorite joke to use at this point is one that makes a reference to email. It is a multiple punch line joke, and I like it so much that instead of waiting until the appropriate section in Part Two, I am including it here. It is called, "The Misdirected Email."

The Misdirected Email

An Illinois man left the snow-filled streets of Chicago for a vacation in Florida. His wife was on a business trip and was planning to meet him there the next day. When he reached his hotel, he decided to send his wife a quick email. Unable to find the scrap of paper on which he had jotted down her email address, he did his best to type it in from memory.

Unfortunately, he missed one letter and his note was directed instead to an elderly woman whose husband had passed away only the day before!"

When the grieving widow checked her email, she took one look at the screen, let out a piercing scream, and fell to the floor in a dead faint.

At the sound, her family rushed into the room and saw this note on the screen:

DEAREST WIFE:

JUST GOT CHECKED IN. [Laugh!]

EVERYTHING PREPARED FOR YOUR ARRIVAL TOMORROW. [Laugh!]

YOUR LOVING HUSBAND [Pause . . .]

P.S. SURE IS HOT DOWN HERE! [Big laugh!]

This joke has three punch lines, each one more hilarious than the preceding one. The last one is especially good for my audiences, because as Christians they believe in heaven and hell, and they can clearly identify with what must have been going through the mind of that poor woman.

Laughing at *Me*!

By the time I finish this joke, I'm always splitting with laughter. Even as I read it, I assume certain facial expressions I have developed that are designed to bring the audience along. I also employ well-rehearsed tones to my voice and vary the cadence of my speech from time to time. In fact, I do this with every joke I tell.

Why some people dead-pan jokes, I'll never know. If you don't think your joke is funny, why should anyone else? How does a blank expression make a joke funnier at the delivery? Not only do I roar at my own jokes, I must admit that I enjoy doing it. Don't forget, laughter begets laughter. Even some of the folks out there who may have a very low humor quotient and who usually don't laugh at jokes begin to laugh solely because I'm laughing. And the joy of laughter, contagious as it is, spreads rapidly through the crowd.

Very often, a stranger will come up to me during a break and say, "Peter, I love your jokes!" Then, moving in closer as if to tell me a secret, he or she continues in a softer voice, "To be honest, we are laughing more at *you* than at your *jokes!*" When I hear this, I'm ecstatic! Apparently, my plan is working! I am meeting my objective: people are laughing and having a good time. Remember, the important thing is not what is making them laugh. What's important is that they are laughing.

Once we have established the mutual expectation that every time I get before the audience we are going to have a fun few minutes, almost anything can provoke a laugh. Even the immediate anticipation of a joke can bring laughter. For example, I frequently pull the joke out of my shirt pocket (some are laughing out loud when I do), scan it, pretend to be elated when I see it, and say, "Wait 'till you hear this one! You're going to love it! Are you ready for this one? Say yes!" They say "Yes!" and they even look at each other and laugh at that, not because it is a punch line, but because they know that we're having fun. And we are!

What Makes Them Laugh?

So what makes people laugh? The joke makes them laugh, I make them laugh, and they make each other laugh! That puts it all in a nutshell.

CHAPTER 4

WHO CAN MAKE PEOPLE LAUGH?

Who can make people laugh? *You* can!

I'm well aware that some of you reading this book will be very skeptical of that statement. As a matter of fact, some of you may even laugh at the very idea that I would suggest that you can make others laugh! After all, you know yourself and your own personality and I probably don't know you at all. At this point you may be saying, "How could I ever make anybody laugh? I've never had much of a sense of humor! I can't tell jokes!"

All of that may indeed be true. Even so, I still maintain that you *can* learn to make people laugh. How do I know? Because for many years I was just like you. I can understand your skepticism about using humor because that was my self-image as well for most of my life. But then I changed my mind and when I did I started making people laugh. Let me explain.

I happen to be writing this in 2005, and consequently I am now on this side of my 75th birthday. Those 75 years divide easily into three periods of 25 years each. I spent the first 25 years getting an education. At the age of 25 I was ordained into the Christian ministry and began my vocation, which has revolved mostly around teaching. That means I have been teaching now for 50 years, but I have been telling jokes for only the last 25 of them.

You see, I grew up in a nice, functional family, but I cannot remember my mother or father ever telling jokes. I do recall that part of our high school culture was for us boys to tell jokes to each other, the great majority of them "dirty" jokes. Not long after graduating from high school I became a born-again Christian and from then on I wanted nothing more to do with dirty jokes. But since almost all the jokes I had ever been exposed to were dirty jokes, I found myself throwing the baby out with the bathwater, so to speak, to the point where I did not like any jokes at all, even clean ones.

A Humorless Teacher!

Consequently, I joined the ranks of those teachers whom we all know by experience. They can teach an entire 10-week course (or even an entire school year) without making the class laugh once. I was one of them. No jokes for me or my students. Jokes were inappropriate in the classroom, particularly in a Christian environment—or so I thought. I became a humorless teacher.

In 1970 I moved to southern California to teach in a theological seminary there. Even though I was humorless, I generally was regarded as a good teacher. Still, I always wanted to do better. It so happened that eventually I developed an association with one of America's most renowned pastors, Robert Schuller of the Crystal Cathedral, and he became my chosen role model as a communicator. Although we were approximately the same age, I wanted to be like Schuller when I "grew up"!

There were many things that contributed to Schuller's legendary communication skills. To my surprise, I discovered that one of the most obvious of these was humor. You mean it was okay to tell jokes in church? Even from the pulpit? And the people responded in a very positive way! My conclusion? If jokes were okay in church, why not in the classroom? I realized that if I was going to improve my communication skills as a teacher, I needed to make my students laugh more. So I decided to work on it.

The Biggest Step

Looking back on it, I now understand that I had just taken the biggest step toward making people laugh. I had decided that I *wanted* to do it! The most difficult part of making any change in our lives is reaching the conscious, deliberate decision *to* change—to *decide* to do something differently.

When I said earlier that *you* can make people laugh, I was assuming that you *want* to make people laugh. Why would I assume this? Because if you have stayed with me and read this far in the book, by now, presumably, you have seen how enjoyable and how healthy it can be to laugh. You understand how laughter can turn out to be fun for you as well as for those around you. So, even though you may not have told many jokes and are still "convinced" you can never tell good jokes, you don't have to keep living like this. The first step toward changing your situation is to decide that you want to *change* it. Do you? Is becoming a better communicator important enough to you to motivate you to step out of your comfort zone and try something new and different that will expand your horizons and enhance your effectiveness?

Now, I'm not saying that you have to be like me. Perish the thought! When I decided that I wanted to be more like Robert Schuller and make my hearers laugh, I knew I could not do it the way Schuller does. Robert Schuller is one of a kind. He has an uncanny ability to tell a story involving a life experience in a way that turns out to be hilarious. I wish I could tell a story like Schuller—and so do about 95% of America's other public speakers! Since I knew that was not a realistic goal for me, I decided to look for an alternative.

It was a process of trial and error and I ended up on many dead end streets. I found myself envying some of my other friends who seemed able to come up with humorous one-liners at will. I would have loved to be able to use irony. I thought of a story I once heard, of British author George Bernard Shaw. Isadora Duncan, the famous dancer, supposedly wrote to Shaw and proposed that they have a child together because, as she said, "It could inherit my beauty and your brains." Shaw replied, "Madam, I am flattered, but suppose it turned out to have my beauty and your brains?"

No, I knew I wasn't up to this quality of humor.

Why not use jokes? Schuller didn't tell them, but I didn't care. Since I didn't have much to lose, I began trying them out in my classes on an occasional basis. It didn't come easy. Predictably, some of my jokes were good, some were mediocre—and some were downright bad. Whenever I found a good one, however, I would try it on another class. It was a learning process. The more I did this, the better I became at evaluating and selecting good jokes.

But this brought to light another problem: I found I had a very difficult time remembering the jokes. In fact, in the beginning I even thought that you had to memorize a joke in order to tell it well. Since I have never been much of a mem- orizer, I began to despair. I did have enough sense to make a list of the jokes I liked, but the list included only brief notes to remind me of the essentials. At least it was a beginning.

Give It a Try!

Maybe you are not a teacher or a public speaker or any- one else who has a captive audience of adults like I have. That doesn't matter. Regardless of who you are or what you do, you have an "audience" of one kind or another, even if it is only occasionally. Try it out. Bring up the idea of jokes dur- ing a break at work or when you go out with others to din- ner. Start the conversation by saying something like, "Hey, I'm reading a book called *Let's Laugh!* It's got some really good jokes. Would you like to hear one of them?" In this way you begin to create what is called the "humor expectation." People laugh best and enjoy it the most when they are prepared for it beforehand. Creating a positive humor expectation is a very important preliminary to making people laugh.

In almost every case, if you're with friends, they will say, "Sure; let's hear it." If you have done your homework, you have photocopied one of the jokes in this book (or any other joke source that you have found) that you liked the best. As you pull the copy of the joke from your pocket, make an excuse for having it written down by saying something like, "I don't want to blow the punch line, so I'm going to go ahead and read it." Raise your audience's expectations a bit by laughing and saying, "I really love this one!" Then read the joke out loud. Try to use a tone of voice that conveys to the other people how much you enjoy reading it to them and reveals your own anticipation of a hilarious punch line, even though you already know the joke. And keep a little smile on your face throughout—anything to communicate subtly that laughter is appropriate and expected. Chances are that when you read the punch line, your friends are going to laugh. Laugh *with* them; don't just sit there with a straight face. Your laughter will make them laugh even more.

I just mentioned *reading* jokes instead of telling memorized ones. Conventional wisdom says that reading jokes will not work. This is absolutely true; reading jokes will not work in some circumstances. Take, for example, professional comedians. They can stand up in front of an audience for twenty minutes and produce twenty minutes of laughter, a good bit of it very hilarious. In most cases it would not work for them to read their jokes. Professional comedy routines are *performances* that are practiced and polished beforehand just as thoroughly as any professional musician would prepare for a concert or recital. Comedians have the ability to memorize their jokes, to create a humor-filled environment and to tell their jokes with just the right expression and timing. These extremely talented people, however, are few and far between, and I am not one of them. So I have to take another approach.

Since I am not a professional comedian but a teacher for whom humor is a means to an end and since I don't tell jokes one after another, it works really well for me to write them out, put them in my shirt pocket and read them one at a time. One additional advantage I have is that I usually emcee serious religious conferences. Normally, when I step onto the platform to introduce the next speaker, some of the people in the audience have been so moved by the previous speaker that they have been crying or at least thinking deeply and working on readjusting things in their lives. They are ready for a break. An emotional change of pace is welcome. That's why so often they look at each other and begin to laugh when I pull the piece of paper out of my pocket. They know a joke is at hand. A moment of levity is coming and they want a few moments of fun before they have to get serious again.

The Dog Food Joke

Yes, I do have a few jokes that I have memorized, but they are ones that I tell on myself. It wouldn't work, for example, if I read from a slip of paper, "I did this" or "I did that." If I am telling a joke on myself I need to have it memorized so as to create the illusion at least that the "story" is something that really happened to me. In fact, one of these memorized jokes comes pretty close to what a professional comedian would do because it has punch line after punch line. I don't use it too often because it takes quite a bit of time—more time than I usually have in any given situation or setting. The title I give to this joke is "Dog Food."

Be aware, however, that this joke is *not* an ice-breaker. In order for it to work, the audience has to know that you like to tell jokes and they need to have laughed at a few already before this one comes up. In order to create the atmosphere for this joke, I start off by saying, "If anybody wonders, my favorite food is what I've never had before. I don't know why I'm like this. Maybe it's because I was a field missionary in Bolivia for sixteen years and I have eaten a lot of strange stuff like monkey, lion, horse, frogs, and grasshoppers... things I never had before."

Then, if I have time, I make a joke out of what I have just said. I pause for a moment, pretend that a new thought has just popped into my mind, and say, "Oh, yeah! There's one more *really* strange one. It is the embryo of an animal still in its birth sac. They cook it only a little bit so it's lukewarm on the inside but still liquid." I pause to let the image sink in "In fact, I had it right here in America!" By this time people in the audience usually are in a state of unbelief. Then I go to the punch line: "They called it a soft-boiled egg!"

All of this is in preparation for the dog food joke. (I told you it would take time!) However, if time is a bit short, I leave it as it is with that outburst of laughter and pick up on the second part the next time I am on the platform.

Second Part

My lead in for the second part is, "For years I have taught on foreign missions in a theological seminary and I now have graduates all over the world. More often than not, when I go to a certain country for whatever reason, one or more of my former students writes me and asks me for a private meeting or for dinner or to meet their family. However, my time is so thinly sliced that I routinely have my staff send apologies...except this one time. I was going to the Philippines a few years ago and I received one of those requests from Emiliano Bermoy. As I have explained, my favorite food is what I've never had before. It suddenly occurred to me that in the Philippines they eat dogs, and I'd never had dog! So I wrote to Emiliano and said that if he could arrange a dog dinner, I'd be glad to meet with him.

"He wrote right back—no problem! So we went out to dinner. Doris was with me. It was a feast because there are three main ways they cook dogs in the Philippines, and he had some cooked all three ways."

Now, with this long build-up we're ready for the first of multiple punch lines. I raise my eyebrows a bit, put the little grin on my face, and say, "We wolfed it down!" The audience laughs and some of them think that is the end. But it isn't!

Right on the heels of the laughter I say, "Then I began to catch on. I saw that one of the menus said: Fettuccine al fido!" That always sparks a new round of laughter and before they can stop, I go on:

"For breakfast you can have beagles & cream cheese. Or if they don't have any of that, pooched eggs!

By this time, everyone, including me, is laughing uproariously. And while still laughing, I say, "You know what the fast food is over there?" Quick pause. "Greyhound!"

After that I let the laughs die down a bit and then say, offhandedly, "The problem is that when you're in a restaurant, you never know if you should ask for a doggie bag!"

At this point, anything I say will make them laugh. So I continue, "Their national anthem over there is "How much is that doggie in the window?"

As the laughter dies down once more, I pretend it's all over. But then, as though it is an after thought, I turn and say, "I came home and told my seminary students about this. One of them was from Hong Kong. A couple of weeks after he graduated, he sent me a cookbook from Hong Kong: *Twenty-one Ways to Wok Your Dog*!" It takes a second or two for them to catch the pun and realize that it is not "walk" but "wok." Even though they're tired of laughing by now, they laugh again. (They simply can't help it!) Finally I say, "That was a delayed action punch line!" Then we settle down for the next serious religious presentation. They are ready!

Puns

If you analyze "The Dog Food Joke" you can see that it consists simply of a string of puns bound together by a simple unifying theme: in this case, that dog is a common food item in the Philippines. Puns are plays on words; they are words that can have a double meaning, depending on how they are used. Some people, like those scientists in England who proposed a formula to rate jokes, think that all puns are terrible and that anyone who is "serious" about humor will never use them. For the most part I would agree. Most of the typical joke books I have read (and I have read many) contain puns that I generally find disgusting as purported examples of humor. Many are off-color and some are downright dirty; others are simply poor humor in my opinion. So let's say that the general rule is not to use puns. Those who say that the pun is the lowest form of wit may be right. However, there are always exceptions to every rule, so do not shy away from puns entirely. But learn to be discerning and selective.

For instance, here is an example of a terrible pun:

A man called the switchboard for a certain party. He was told that the party's extension was 4-8-2. He said, "That sounds like a cannibal story to me!"

This one is even worse:

A panda walks into a bar, eats a hamburger, then pulls out a gun and shoots the waiter. The owner rushes up and says, "What's going on? You just shot my waiter and you didn't pay for the food!" The panda looks back and says, "Hey, I'm a panda. Just look it up!" So the owner gets out his dictionary and reads, "A panda is a tree-climbing mammal of Asian origin, characterized by distinct black and white coloring. Eats shoots and leaves."

And here, on the other hand, is a great pun:

Did you hear what the Mexican firefighter named his two sons? Hose A and Hose B!

The listener, of course, does not at first hear "Hose A," but rather "José." The "Hose B" is a complete surprise. This is not an ethnic joke that puts anyone down. It is simply having good fun with a harmless play on words.

You Can Make People Laugh!

If you have hung in there with me to this point of the book, you may be more open to making people laugh than you were before. It may also be a sign that you have a better sense of humor than you think you do. I hope both are true of you. People with a low tolerance for humor either do not understand jokes or quickly become bored or exasperated with them. The fact that you are still here proves there is hope for you yet! You *can* make people laugh!

Let me summarize quickly some of the things I have said by giving you a simple checklist. These are time- and experience-tested principles that, if followed, soon will have you making people laugh. Once you start, I don't think you'll ever get tired of it!

☛ **Believe that it is possible for you to tell jokes.** Chances are that by now you do believe that you can do it. If you still have some doubts, keep in mind that certain types of jokes will work better for you than others. Experiment until you find the kind of jokes that work for you.

☞ **Decide that you want to tell jokes and make people laugh.** Following this checklist will require time, energy and effort on your part. Before you begin, make sure that telling jokes to make people laugh is really what you want to do. It all depends on whether or not you want to become a more effective teacher and/or communicator. If you are not really interested in becoming a joke-teller, then for you following this checklist will not be worth the necessary effort.

☞ **Make a joke file.** If you think you're going to remember the jokes you hear, you'll be disappointed. Memory can be a fickle thing, particularly as you grow older. When you hear a good joke, write it down immediately. Keep some blank paper and a pencil in your pocket or purse. Be sure to write down the punch line. Recently, when I reviewed my own joke file in preparation for writing this book, I was appalled at the number of jokes I had jotted down by title but have since forgotten the punch line! I assumed back then that I would remember such a great punch line, but no such luck. If you read a joke you like, as I hope you will in this book, tear it out or photocopy it for your file. Decide on your favorite categories and sort out your jokes. If you have a computer, set up a folder with separate files for each category of joke. Update your file regularly. There's always room for fresh material.

☞ **Find an audience.** Start where you are. Who are the people you are with on a regular basis who could become your audience? Family members? Work colleagues? Fellow church members? I predict that once you start trying, you will have less problem in finding people who want to listen to your jokes than you might have thought possible.

☞ **Test your jokes by reading them.** This doesn't apply so much to one-liners, but it does to most jokes. Get over the idea that people won't laugh at a joke that you read. If it's a good joke, and if you deliver it well, they will—even if you read it.

☞ **Develop an environment of humor.** As you begin to tell your joke, cultivate a personal attitude of playfulness. Expect to have fun. The others will have more fun if you are having fun. When you're reading your joke, smile! I repeat, smile! Try to get a little chuckle in your voice as you approach the punch line. The more you do this, the more you will develop skills of emphasis, timing, pausing, and speed of delivery. It takes practice, as do all things that are worth doing, but practice will pay off in big dividends of laughter, fun and increased effectiveness.

☞ **Cull your jokes.** The first time you tell a joke, look at it as an experiment. You are deciding if it is a keeper or not. Don't lose heart if people don't laugh at a joke. They might have heard it before. Caution: never start a joke with "Have you heard the one about da-da-da?" Just assume it is new for them, and if they tell you they've heard it, that's okay. Say, "It's a good one, isn't it?" Believe in the humor of your own jokes or you will easily become discouraged. At the same time, be realistic. If a joke bombs, as some inevitably will do, spend some time trying to figure out *why* the joke bombed. Was it the wrong joke for that particular audience? Was your timing off? Did you make a mistake in delivery? Or was it simply a bad joke? If that is the case, toss it, especially if you try it on another audience and it bombs again!

☛ **Gain a reputation.** It won't happen overnight, but if you are diligent in applying this checklist, eventually people will expect you to tell jokes. Once you have gained this reputation, you are over the hump. I can promise you that from that point on, you will enjoy life more than you ever have before.

You can make people laugh!

PART TWO

THE BEST JOKES
AND WHY THEY ARE!

BLONDE JOKES

Why am I starting with blonde jokes? It is because I want to demonstrate the principle of selectivity.

In all the reading I have done on humor, I have never seen anyone try to estimate the number of jokes out there, and with good reason. The number of jokes isn't infinite, but it comes pretty close. *Reader's Digest* probably holds the record for publishing the most jokes of any periodical. Bookstores carry shelves of joke books. Enormous quantities of jokes are passed around by word of mouth. And now that the Internet has emerged, the joke supply has multiplied exponentially.

I say this to affirm that anyone interested in humor, from people who enjoy an occasional laugh to those of us who tell jokes as a part of our vocation, needs to be selective. No one has ever read or heard all the jokes that exist. Which ones should we read? Which ones should we discard? Which ones should we keep?

The obvious answer is that we should keep the jokes that are funny (and clean) and toss the ones that are not. But how can we tell the difference? And how do we determine which jokes are right for us and for the particular types of audiences we will encounter?

Probably no two people will give the same answers to those questions. That is because, as we saw in chapter 3, different people laugh at different things. Take, for example, the average paperback joke book that you might find on the newsstand in an airport. The compiler of that book obviously used the principle of selectivity. He or she chose the funniest jokes out of a huge reservoir of humor. But here is the strange thing: I have read a number of those books from cover to cover, and in more than one I did not find a single joke that I thought was funny enough to tell from the platform.

Does this mean my standards of acceptability and funniness are too high? Not necessarily. I do have high standards for the jokes I use, but my failure to find the humor in the jokes in most joke books may simply reflect differences of taste between myself and the authors of those books.

This is one reason why the principle of selectivity is so important. Just because a joke has been published in a joke book—even a best-selling joke book—does not mean necessarily that is a good or appropriate joke for you in your particular circumstances. You must be very selective, considering both your own personality as well as the probable makeup of the audiences you are most likely to encounter.

In this section you will find the jokes that I happen to think are funny. But I am not presumptuous enough to assume that you will feel the same way. However, I have enough experience in this area to make the confident prediction that no matter who you are, you will find at least a few jokes that will tickle your funny bone! If you don't, that's okay but there is little more I can do to help you.

In my opinion, everyone's joke selection process should include the rejection of jokes that are mean. I have already suggested that jokes that put down an individual or a group are distasteful, even though they might be funny. I will mention several other reasons for rejecting jokes as time goes by, but for the moment, let's focus on the put downs.

Blonde jokes are classic put downs. Some of the worst jokes I have seen are also among the most typical and popular blonde jokes. How the idea ever arose that women with blonde hair could be dumber than women with other colors of hair, to say nothing of men, is a complete mystery to me. In every blonde joke, the blonde loses, usually by making a jackass out of herself through an incredibly stupid remark in the punch line. I hate blonde jokes! I have no doubt that over the years I have thrown away no less than 500 blonde jokes, and I plan to throw away 500 more.

However, strange as it may seem, I tell blonde jokes frequently. And I get great laughs. In fact, the blondes in the audience laugh the hardest of all. I don't recall ever bombing with my blonde jokes. So what's going on?

Once again, it is the principle of selectivity. I select blonde jokes that not only are funny but jokes in which the blonde always wins! The blondes in my jokes do not emerge as the goat but as the hero. I haven't found many of them, but I do have a half dozen or so.

Here's what I always say before I tell my first blonde joke: "Look around you and see how many blondes there are out there. I want to talk to you blondes. I know that you have had it up to here with blonde jokes. I don't blame you. Some of the most horrible jokes in all of America are blonde jokes. When I get them, I throw them away by the tons. I hate blonde jokes!" By this time I have their full attention, both blondes and non-blondes alike. Then I say, "Except for five of them!" This always gets a laugh and sparks their interest even further. In fact, at this point, many are challenging me, wondering how I, or anyone else, could possibly tell a decent blonde joke. So I say, "I'll tell you the difference. In my jokes the blonde always wins!" Okay. This helps. Now they want to see if I can pull it off.

I like to tell the one about the blonde and the lawyer first because it radically reverses stereotypes. Our stereotype of lawyers is that they're very smart and our stereotype of blondes is that they're very dumb. Watch how this turns things around:

The Blonde and the Lawyer

A blonde and a lawyer are sitting next to each other on a flight from Los Angeles to New York. The lawyer asks if she would like to play a fun game.

The blonde, who's tired, just wants to take a nap. She politely declines and rolls over to the window to catch a few winks. The lawyer persists and explains that the game is easy and a lot of fun. He explains, "I ask you a question, and if you don't know the answer, you pay me $5.00 and vice versa." Again the blonde declines and tries to get some sleep.

The lawyer, now agitated, says, "Okay, if you don't know the answer you pay me $5.00. But if I don't know the answer, I'll pay you $500!

Well, this catches the blonde's attention and, figuring there will be no end to this torment unless she plays, agrees to the game. The lawyer asks the first question: "What's the distance from the earth to the moon?" The blonde doesn't say a word, reaches into her purse, pulls out a $5.00 bill, and hands it to the lawyer.

"Okay," says the lawyer, "your turn." She asks the lawyer, "What goes up a hill with three legs and comes down with four legs?" The lawyer, puzzled, takes out his laptop computer and searches all his references. No answer. He taps into the air phone with his modem and searches the net and the Library of Congress. No answer. Frustrated, he sends emails to all his friends and coworkers, but to no avail.

After an hour, he wakes up the blonde and hands her $500. The blonde says, "Thank you," and turns back to get some more sleep. The lawyer, who is now more than a little miffed, wakes up the blonde and asks, "Well, what's the answer?" Without a word, the blonde reaches into her purse, hands the lawyer $5.00, and goes back to sleep!

The laughter starts when the blonde reaches into her purse because that's when some of the brightest in the audience catch on to what's happening. It increases when the $5.00 comes out, and then peaks when she goes back to sleep. The blonde wins and the lawyer loses. This doesn't put down the lawyer either, as many lawyer jokes do. Why not? Because it was the lawyer's game; he made the rules and the blonde simply played by the rules. Everybody loves the blonde!

Let me remind you that, unlike comedians who pursue laughs for their own sake, I do not tell a bunch of jokes one right after the other. I tell a joke or two at the beginning of each new session in a conference or at the beginning of a class in a classroom and after each break.

After an hour or two of paying close attention to some rather heavy or challenging content, the hearers are always ready for a mental break. Now that I've given them one good blonde joke, they are eager to hear more. So at this point, I simply pull the paper out of my pocket and say, "Here's another one of those blonde jokes." When I do, I usually get a mixture of shouts and applause encouraging me to go ahead.

The $5,000 Loan

A blonde walks into a bank in New York City and asks for the loan officer. She says she's going to Europe on a business trip for two weeks and she needs to borrow $5,000. The bank officer says that they will need some kind of security for the loan, so the blonde hands over the keys to a new Rolls Royce. The car is parked out in front of the bank, she has the title, and everything checks out. The bank agrees to accept the car as collateral for the loan.

The bank's president and its officers all enjoy a good laugh at this blonde for using a $250,000 Rolls Royce as collateral against a $5,000 loan. An employee of the bank then proceeds to drive the Rolls into the bank's underground garage and parks it there.

Two weeks later, the blonde returns, repays the $5,000, along with the interest, which comes to $15.41. The loan officer says, "Miss, we are very happy to have had your business, and this transaction has worked out very nicely. But we're a little puzzled. You see, while you were away we did a background check and found that you are a multi-millionaire. What puzzles us is why you would bother to borrow $5,000?"

With a smile, the blonde replies, "Where else in New York City can I park my car in a perfectly safe place for two weeks for only $15.41?"

One thing that helps this joke is the implied agreement among the bank employees that their blonde customer is another one of those "dumb blondes" when she uses the Rolls as collateral. The hearers usually begin to catch the punch line with the words "park my car," and by the time I finish, the laughter is typically so loud that many never hear the "$15.41" at the end. They don't care!

The next joke combines a blonde joke with a religious joke. This is particularly useful to me, since my audiences are made up of evangelical Christian believers. So before I tell the joke, I say to the audience, "Here's another blonde joke. This one is the most religious of all." They usually can't wait to hear it.

Three Singapore Slings

A blonde walks into a barroom and orders three Singapore Slings. She sits in the back of the room drinking a sip out of each one in turn. When she finishes them, she comes back to the bar and orders three more.

The bartender approaches her and says, "You know, a Singapore Sling goes flat after I make it and it sits for a long time. It would taste better if you bought only one at a time."

The blonde replies, "Well, you see, I have two sisters. One is in England and the other is in Australia, and I'm here in the United States. When we all parted from our home, we promised that we'd drink this way to remember the days when we drank together. So I drink one for each of my sisters and one for myself." The bartender admits that this is a nice custom, and leaves it there.

The blonde becomes a regular in the bar and always drinks the same way. She orders three Singapore Slings and drinks them in turn.

One day she comes in and orders two Singapore Slings. All the other regulars take notice and fall silent. When she comes back to the bar for the second round, the bartender says, "I don't want to intrude on your grief, but I wanted to offer my condolences on your great loss."

The blonde looks confused for a moment, then a light dawns in her eyes and she laughs. "Oh, no! Everyone's fine," she explains. "It's just that last week I joined a Baptist Church and I had to quit drinking!"

This one works for my people because they all know that Baptists traditionally are teetotalers. A good number of them are ex-Baptists, and many feel that total abstinence from alcohol stretches Christian legalism a bit too far. For the blonde suddenly to be a Baptist who still drinks Singapore Slings is hilarious!

The next one is a cross over. I probably should put it in my category of Religious Jokes, but since the winner is a blonde, I have decided to include it here. This has everything that a joke could ask for. It's probably one of my top ten.

Sister Helen

Two priests decided to go to Hawaii on vacation. They determined to make it a real vacation by not wearing anything that would identify them as clergy.

As soon as the plane landed, they headed for a store and bought some really outrageous trunks, sunglasses, shirts, and whatever.

The next morning they went to the beach, dressed in their "tourist" garb. They were sitting on beach chairs, enjoying a drink, when a gorgeous blonde in a bikini came walking straight towards them. They couldn't help but stare.

As the blonde passed them, she smiled and said, "Good morning, Father; good morning, Father," addressing each of them individually, then she went on by.

They were both stunned. How in heaven's name did she know they were priests?

The next day they went back to the store and bought even more outrageous outfits. Once again, they settled on the beach in their chairs to enjoy the sunshine. After a while, the same gorgeous blonde came walking toward them. Again, she approached them and greeted each one individually, "Good morning, Father; good morning, Father," and started to walk away.

One of the priests couldn't stand it any longer and he said, "Just a minute, young lady!"

"Yes?" she replied.

"Look, it's true we are priests, and we're proud of it. But I have to know, young lady, how in the world did you know we are priests?

"Oh, Father," she said, "It's me, Sister Helen!"

This is a Catholic joke but it doesn't make fun of a religion; it sets up an incredibly humorous situation which doesn't violate any Catholic principles. The hearers roar at the mental image of a blonde nun in a bikini. But why not? What's good for the goose is good for the gander. If the priests could wear beach clothing, why not the nun? Sister Helen is totally innocent. It's just that hardly anyone even tries to imagine what is there under that religious habit, but, when you think of it, it could look good in a bikini!

This last blonde joke isn't quite a good as the first four. But it will work, especially when the audience has laughed at several blonde jokes.

Jonah in Heaven?

A blonde business traveler, who was a believer, customarily read her Bible on long flights. This time she was sitting next to an apparently dignified gentleman in a suit and tie, reading the *Wall Street Journal*.

They were minding their own business until she took out her Bible and started reading. That caught the man's attention, and he chuckled a bit under his breath.

After a while, he turned to the blonde and said, "You don't really believe all that stuff in there, do you?"

"Of course I do," she said. "It's the Bible."

"How about that guy who was supposed to be swallowed by a whale?"

"Yes, I believe that. It's in the Bible."

"Look. Tell me something. How do you suppose he survived all that time inside a whale?"

"To be truthful," the blonde said, "I don't know. Maybe when I get to Heaven, I'll ask him."

The man laughed sarcastically. "What if he's not in Heaven?"

"Well," the blonde said, "Then *you* can ask him!"

Some People Just Don't Understand

I can't recall how many times I have gone through this routine of blonde jokes, underscoring the fact that what makes a blonde joke good is that the blonde wins, but I constantly run into people who don't seem to get it. Time after time people will email me with words to the effect, "Peter, here's a blonde joke you will love. I know you'll add it to your collection!" I hate to insert a bad joke into this book, but I'm going to do it just to show what I mean by a bad blonde joke. This is one that a friend actually emailed me.

A blonde calls her boyfriend and says, "Please come over and help me. I have a killer jigsaw puzzle, and I can't figure out how to get it started.

Her boyfriend asks, "What is it supposed to be when it is finished?" The blonde says, "According to the picture on the box, it's a tiger. Her boyfriend decides to go over and help with the puzzle. She lets him in and shows him where she has the puzzle spread all over the table. He takes one look at the pieces and the box, and then turning to her he says, "Sweetheart, first of all no matter what we do, we're not going to put these pieces together to make a tiger." Then he takes her hand and says, "And secondly, I want you to relax. Let's have a nice cup of tea, and then let's put all these Frosted Flakes back in the box!"

Yuck! Can you imagine a worse joke? The blonde isn't just dumb, she's an imbecile. Furthermore, no one on this planet would key in to the set up. Please don't email me jokes like this!

WORKPLACE JOKES

This category of workplace jokes is likely more important for me that it might be for you. Because I deal primarily with the religious community, I of course would have many religious jokes. They are coming later. But I also wrote a book called *The Church in the Workplace*, which gives me an excuse for saying to an audience, "Ever since I have written that book, I started to collect workplace jokes!" Since I have established the reputation as a joke teller, this helps create the environment for humor that I have frequently mentioned.

At times, I use a one-liner as a throw away. When the audience is expecting a full-blown joke, I will say something like, "This isn't the real joke, but you're still going to love it!" Then I tell it:

Noah the Businessman

Do you know why Noah went down as the best businessman in the Bible? Because he floated all his assets while the rest of the world was in liquidation!

Because this is a pun, it draws a combination of good-hearted groans as well as some laughs. But its purpose is only a lead in to whatever joke I decide to tell next.

This next one is a workplace joke with a religious over-tone, so it fits my audiences well:

The Bible on the Beach

A businessman was in a great deal of trouble. His business was failing. He had put everything he had into the business. He owed everybody. It was so bad he was even contemplating suicide.

As a last resort he went to a pastor and poured out his story of tears and woe. When he had finished, the pastor said, "Here's what I want you to do: Put a beach chair and your Bible in your car and drive down to the beach. Take the beach chair and the Bible to the water's edge. Sit down in the beach chair, and put the Bible on your lap. Open the Bible, the wind will rifle the pages, but finally the open Bible will come to rest on a page. Look down at the page and read the first thing you see. That will be your answer. That will tell you what to do."

A year later the businessman drove back to the pastor in his brand new BMW, dressed in a new cus-tom-tailored suit. He pulled an envelope stuffed with money from his pocket and gave it to the pastor in thanks for his advice. The pastor was curious. "You did as I suggested?" he asked.

"Absolutely," replied the businessman.

"You went to the beach?"

"Absolutely."

"You sat on a beach chair and opened a Bible on your lap?"

"Absolutely."

"You let the pages rifle in the wind until they stopped?"

"Absolutely."

"And what were the first words that you saw?"

"Chapter 11!"

Donkey Raffle

A city boy named Percy moved to the country. He bought a donkey from a farmer for $100. The farmer agreed to deliver the donkey the next day, but when he arrived, he said, "I'm sorry, but the donkey died last night."

"Well, O.K.," said Percy. Just give me my money back."

"I can't," said the farmer. "I already spent it."

"O.K.," said Percy. "At least give me the donkey."

"What are you going to do with a dead donkey?" asked the farmer.

"I'm going to raffle it off."

"Raffle off a dead donkey?"

"Sure, I just won't tell anyone he's dead."

A month later the farmer met up with Percy. "What happened with the dead donkey?"

"I raffled him off. I sold 500 tickets at $2.00 a piece, and I made a profit of $898."

"Didn't anybody complain?" asked the farmer.

"Just the guy who won. So I gave him his two dollars back!"

The M.I.T. Job Applicant

Reaching the end of a job interview, the Human Resources Officer asked a young engineer, fresh out of M.I.T., "And what starting salary were you looking for?"

The engineer replies, "In the region of $125,000 a year, depending on the benefits package."

The interviewer inquires, "Well, what would you say to a package of 5 weeks vacation, 14 paid holidays, full medical and dental, company matching retirement fund to 50% of salary, and a company car leased new every 2 years, say a red Corvette?"

The engineer sits up straight in his chair and says, "Wow! Are you kidding?"

The interviewer replies, "Yeah, but you started it!"

The Most Famous Man?

One day in the second-grade of an international school, the teacher said to the class of 7-year-olds, "I'll give $2.00 to the child who can tell me who was the most famous man who ever lived.

An Irish boy put up his hand and said, "It was St. Patrick." The teacher said, "I'm sorry, Sean, but that's not correct."

Then a Scottish boy put up his hand and said, "It was St. Andrew." The teacher said, "I'm sorry, Hamish, but that's not right either."

Finally, a Jewish boy raised his hand and said, "It was Jesus Christ." The teacher said, "That's absolutely right, Michael. Come up here and I'll give you the two dollars." As the teacher was handing Michael his money, she said, "You know, Michael, since you're Jewish, I was very surprised that you said Jesus Christ." Michael replied, "Yeah, in my heart I knew it was Moses, but business is business!"

This is one of those ethnic jokes that is clearly non-offensive. Each boy positively represents his ethnic group and no one is put down. Michael, the Jewish boy, does well also and exhibits a well-known positive characteristic of Jewish people: their ingrained sense of good business, which can start as early as second grade. Notice that Michael played by the rules and won, and everyone ends up loving Michael.

The Boy Entrepreneur (Speeding Trap)

A police officer had a perfect hiding place for watching for speeders. Every day he was there he would make the city a lot of money in fines.

But one day everybody who passed the cop was driving under the speed limit. What was going on? The officer soon discovered the problem. A ten-year-old born entrepreneur was standing on the side of the road with a huge hand-painted sign that read: "RADAR TRAP AHEAD."

A little more investigative work led the officer to the entrepreneur's business partner, another boy his age about 100 yards beyond the radar trap with a hand-painted sign reading: "TIPS HERE," and a bucket at his feet full of bills and change!

Tell this one at a time when you do not need particularly hilarious laughter. The unlikely, surprising scenario itself, which apparently doesn't break any laws but plays a practical joke on the cop, is what draws the response and the mild level of laughter. The net result is that people feel good about it and they're glad you told the story.

This next one is the same type of joke that businesspeople love because it teaches a good lesson. You'll find people asking you for this joke because they know someone they want to teach the lesson to. My suggestion is that you tell them to buy the book!

The Mexican Fisherman

A boat docked in a tiny Mexican village. An American tourist complimented the Mexican fisherman on the quality of his fish and asked how long it took him to catch them.

"Not very long," answered the Mexican.

"But then, why didn't you stay out longer and catch more?" asked the American.

The Mexican explained that his small catch was sufficient to meet his needs and those of his family.

The American asked, "But what do you do with the rest of your time?"

"I sleep late, fish a little, play with my children, and take a siesta with my wife. In the evenings, I go into the village to see my friends, have a few drinks, play the guitar, and sing a few songs. I have a full life."

The American interrupted, "Look," he said, "I have an MBA from Harvard and I can help you! You should start by fishing longer every day. You can then sell the extra fish you catch. With the extra revenue, you can buy a bigger boat."

"And after that?" asked the Mexican.

"With the extra money the larger boat will bring, you can buy a second one and a third one and so on until you have an entire fleet of trawlers. Instead of selling your fish to a middle man, you can then negotiate directly with the processing plants and maybe even open your own plant. You can then leave this little village and move to Mexico City, Los Angeles, or even New York City!

From there you can direct your huge new enterprise."

"How long would that take?" asked the Mexican.

"Twenty, perhaps twenty-five years," replied the American, "But you'd be making millions!"

"Millions? Wow! And after that?"

"After that you'll be able to retire, live in a tiny village near the coast, sleep late, play with your children, catch a few fish, take a siesta with your wife and spend your evenings drinking and enjoying your friends!"

This next joke I tailored to tell on myself, so naturally I have it memorized. Marketplace people love it. You can tailor it to fit your own needs.

The $5000 Dog

When I lived in California and was teaching in seminary, I was backing out of the driveway one morning on my way to work. There on the lawn of the house next door was the little boy who lived there standing next to a big cardboard box. In the box was a mangy, scroungy dog, and above the box was a sign: DOG FOR SALE: 50¢.

When I came home that afternoon, there was the boy with a dejected look on his face. I went over to him and said, "I see you didn't sell your dog." "No, I didn't," he said. "Would you like some help?" I asked. "Oh, yes. Please." So I said, "O.K. Put the dog away for now and get a good night's sleep. Tomorrow get up early and give your dog a bath. Wash him with good shampoo, blow dry him, and put a red ribbon around his neck. Put him back in the box, but this time, don't put up a sign that says: DOG FOR SALE: 50¢. Nobody wants a 50¢ dog! Put a price on him that's really worth something!"

The next morning I was backing out of the driveway, and sure enough. There was the boy with the dog in the box all washed, blow dried and a red ribbon around his neck. And there was a big sign over the box: DOG FOR SALE: $5,000!.

I came home that afternoon, and I couldn't believe it. There was a sign over the box: SOLD! So I went over and knocked on the door. The boy came to the door with a big smile on his face, and I said, "I see you sold your dog." "Yes, Mr. Wagner," he said. "Thanks for your help." "Well, you're welcome," I said. "But did you really sell him for $5,000?" "Oh, yes, and I never could have done it without you."

Puzzled, I replied, "Well then, tell me, how did you do it?" "Oh," he said. "It was easy. I traded him for two $2,500 cats!"

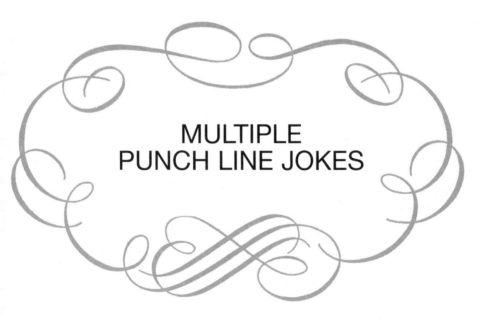

MULTIPLE
PUNCH LINE JOKES

P rofessional comedians have the ability to serve up a regular diet of multiple punch lines. The rest of us have to be satisfied with one joke, one punch line. However, there are exceptions, and I try to use them as frequently as I can because everybody has so much fun with them. Back in Chapter 3, I told the joke about the man in Florida who mistakenly sent the email to a new widow, ending up with "It sure is hot down here!" I like that one for an initial joke because it ends up with three punch lines, each one funnier than the last.

I think it would be accurate to say that this next joke is my best one of all. I get more positive comments on it than any other. And I even regularly get requests from people who have been in my audiences before to repeat it. Those who have heard it two or three times before still laugh just as hard the next time!

Naming the Computer

A language instructor was explaining to her class that in Spanish, nouns, unlike their English counterparts, are grammatically designated as masculine or feminine. For instance, "house" in Spanish is feminine: "la casa." "Pencil" in Spanish is masculine: "el lápiz."

One puzzled student asked, "What gender is 'computer?'" The teacher didn't know, and the word wasn't in her Spanish dictionary. So for fun she split the class into two groups, appropriately enough by gender, and asked them to decide whether "computer" should be a masculine or feminine noun.

Both groups were required to give four reasons for their recommendation. The men's group decided that computers should definitely be of the feminine gender ("la computer") because:

No one but their creator understands their internal logic!

The native language they use to communicate with other computers is incomprehensible to everyone else!

Even the smallest mistakes are stored in long-term memory for possible later retrieval!

As soon as you make a commitment to one, you find yourself spending half your paycheck on accessories for it!

The women's group, however, concluded that computers should be masculine ("el computer") because:

In order to get their attention, you have to turn them on!

They have a lot of data, but they are still clueless!

They are supposed to help you solve problems, but half the time they are the problem!

As soon as you make a commitment to one, you realize that if you'd waited a little longer, you could have gotten a better model!

The women won!

What makes that joke funny to a typical audience is that you create dueling genders. The men lead the laughter on the first four punch lines, especially the one about storing mistakes in long-term memory. The women join them because the lines are really funny. But by now, the women are feeling a little bit on the defensive and they are wondering how anything more could be that funny. And some of the men are even feeling a little sorry for the women. However, the last four punch lines end up even funnier than the first four and everybody's happy. In fact they are usually laughing so loudly that I consistently have trouble in getting in the final line, "The women won!" When I do, they laugh again at that one, too!

Computers vs. Cars

This joke has some similarities to the last one. It doesn't work too well with senior citizens, but it does with a younger crowd that is more techie.

At a famous computer expo, Bill Gates reportedly compared the computer industry with the automobile industry, and he stated: "If GM had kept up with technology like the computer industry has, we would all be driving $25.00 cars that got 1,000 miles to the gallon!"

The people at General Motors were really upset when they heard this. So they issued a press release stating: "If GM had developed technology like Microsoft, we would all be driving cars with the following characteristics:

For no reason whatsoever, your car would crash every day or two!

Occasionally your car would die on the freeway for no reason. You would have to pull over to the side of the road, close all the windows, shut off the car, restart it and reopen the windows before you could continue. For some reason, you would simply accept this!

The oil, water temperature, and alternator warning lights would all be replaced by a single "This Car Has Performed An Illegal Operation" warning light!

The airbag system would ask, "Are you sure?" before deploying!

From time to time, for no reason whatsoever, your car would lock you out and refuse to let you in until you simultaneously lifted the door handle, turned the key, and grabbed hold of the radio antenna!

Forrest Gump in Heaven

Forrest Gump died and went to heaven. At the pearly gates he met St. Peter who told him that new rules were in effect due to the advances in education on earth, and that admittance required the heavenly soul not only to have lived a good life, but also to answer three questions:

Name two days of the week that begin with the letter "T."

How many seconds are there in a year?

What's God's first name?

Forrest thought and thought and said, "I know. The two days of the week that begin with the letter "T" are today and tomorrow!"

St. Peter said that although that was not the answer he was expecting, he would allow it.

Then Forrest said, "There are twelve seconds in every year."

St. Peter gulped. "Okay, how do you figure there are only twelve seconds in a year?

Forrest replied, "January 2nd, February 2nd, March 2nd, .. ."

"Okay, okay," said St. Peter. "I'll give you that one, too! What about the third question?"

Forrest thought some more. "Well, the first name of God is either Andy or Howard."

"And just how did you arrive at those names?" St. Peter asked.

"You know," replied Forrest. "From the song, Andy walks with me, Andy talks with me, Andy tells me I am his own."

Then he added, "And from the prayer, Our Father who art in Heaven, Howard be your name!"

St. Peter welcomed him in without another word!

WWJD?

Most people think that WWJD means "What would Jesus do?"

But what it really means is "What would Jesus drive?"

One theory is that the divine vehicle would be an old Plymouth because the Bible says, "God drove Adam and Eve out of the Garden of Eden in a Fury!"

But in Psalm 83, the Almighty clearly has both a Pontiac and a Geo in his 2-car garage. The passage urges the Lord to "Pursue your enemies with your Tempest and terrify them with your Storm!"

For His pickup truck, God obviously favors a Dodge. Moses' followers are warned not to go up the mountain "until the Ram's horn sounds a long blast!"

Some scholars insist that Jesus drove a Honda, even though He didn't like to talk about it. As proof, they cite a verse in St. John's Gospel where Christ tells the crowd, "For I did not speak of my own Accord!"

Which means that after Jesus left, the apostles probably started car-pooling in His Honda, because it says, "The Apostles were in one Accord!"

Church Bulletin Bloopers

Church bulletin bloopers have become classic humor. When they first started coming out, I think around the 1970s, the sources insisted that they were real errors in real church bulletins. I could not doubt that some were. In fact I have found one or two good ones myself. But I suspect that the great majority of them could be traced to the minds of clever humorists if such tracing were possible.

It doesn't matter. They are still funny. Tons of them are sent around by email. I have tossed out most of those I have read, but I still have a long list of what I consider keepers. As I have said, my audiences are religious people, which is a plus for these jokes. However, most Americans have been to church enough to know a little bit about church culture and that is all that is really needed to see the fun in the bloopers.

When I am going to read bloopers, I prep the audience by asking "How many of you go to churches that pass out an announcement bulletin on Sundays?" Just about everyone raises their hand. Then I ask, "Have you ever found a mistake in one of them?" They look at each other, nod their heads, and smile knowingly. I say, "If you find one, please give it to me. I collect them!" And I show them the list I have in my hand. By now they know what is coming and they're laughing a little with each other in anticipation, even those who have heard similar things before.

I begin by getting them off guard with this one. It does not have a humorous punch line, but it is definitely a curious, almost unexplainable mistake:

☞ Bend, Oregon

Under "SPORTS NEWS:" Basketball at Hillside will restart this Saturday at 5:30 p.m. Bring your softball glove if interested.

That one, out of a real bulletin that I have in my file, doesn't get a hearty laugh, but it does get some surprised chuckles. Then I quickly say, "This one came from my daughter's church in Cheyenne, Wyoming:"

👉 Cheyenne, Wyoming

If you would like a record of your *thighs* and offerings, please see an usher.

When you pronounce "thighs" well enough so the listeners do not hear "tithes," they laugh so quickly that it is difficult for many to hear "please see an usher" but those who hear it laugh even more.

Notice that I have attached a city and state to each of these. None that come in over email have this, but it helps immensely. I just made up the cities and states, except for my daughter's church in Cheyenne, Wyoming. Even though the bloopers may be fictitious, saying the name of a city and state before each one creates a façade of credibility.

I have more bloopers in this list than you would want to use at one time, so select the ones you want. Try to go on long enough, but not too long. Once or twice I tried reading them in two parts, but that doesn't work well. To read some once, and then a while later read some more ends up rather flat the second time around. I don't recommend it.

👉 Hartford, Connecticut

This afternoon there will be a meeting in the south and north ends of the church. Children will be baptized at both ends.

☞ Birmingham, Alabama

Tuesday at 4:00 P.M., there will be an ice cream social. All ladies giving milk, come early.

☞ De Moines, Iowa

This being Easter Sunday, we will ask Mrs. Johnson to come forward and lay an egg on the altar.

☞ Queensville, South Dakota

Ladies, don't forget the rummage sale. It's a good chance to get rid of those things not worth keeping around the house. Bring your husbands.

☞ Perkinsville, Arkansas

The rosebud on the altar this morning is to announce the birth of David Alan Belser, the *sin* of Rev. and Mrs. Julius Belser.

Be sure they hear that word "sin," not "son."

☞ Oneonta, New York

Thursday, at 5:00 p.m., there will be a meeting of the Little Mother's Club. All those wishing to become Little Mothers, please meet the pastor in his study.

☞ Dallas, Texas

The ladies of the church have cast off clothing of every kind, and they may be seen in the basement on Friday afternoon.

☞ Chicago, Illinois

This was a misprint. The final hymn for the benediction was supposed to be "Our God Reigns." However, the bulletin announced that they would sing: "Our God Resigns!"

☞ Sandusky, Ohio

Men's Fellowship: This Saturday the annual bean supper will be held in Fellowship Hall. Music will follow.

☞ Broken Arrow, Oklahoma

Please remember in prayer those who are sick of our church and our community.

☞ Santa Fe, New Mexico

The Pastor would appreciate it if the ladies of the congregation would lend him their electric *girdles* for the pancake breakfast Saturday morning.

☞ **Century Village, Florida**

Weight Watchers will meet at 7:00 P.M. Tuesday. Please use the large double door at the side entrance.

☞ **Shawnee, Oklahoma**

The choir invites any member of the congregation who enjoys sinning to join the choir.

☞ **Eastlake, Michigan**

Eight new choir robes are currently needed, due to the addition of several new choir members and to the deterioration of some older ones.

☞ **Minneapolis, Minnesota**

Our youth basketball team is leading the Lutheran League once again. Come out Wednesday night and watch us kill Christ the King.

☞ **Winter Haven, Florida**

You are encouraged to attend this week's National Prayer & Fasting Conference in Orlando. The registration fee includes meals.

RELIGIOUS JOKES

Since, as I have mentioned several times, I am a Christian minister and my audiences, whether in the classroom or in the auditorium or in the sanctuary are made up of Christian people, it would be expected that my section on religious jokes would be one of the largest. My listeners love religious jokes, so long as they do not put any faith down and so long as they reflect good taste in dealing with religious themes. Religious jokes can backfire if they give any evidence of being sacrilegious.

I usually prep the audience by saying, "A while ago I wrote a book on the spirit of religion. Ever since then I've been collecting religious jokes!" Granted, this is more or less an in-house subject, but my listeners for the most part have decided that they don't want to be associated with the spirit of religion. They want to be Christian believers without being religious. They want to laugh at "religion," which they see as different from laughing at true Christian faith. So they laugh at the idea of religious jokes.

Then I say, "One thing that the spirit of religion hates is for people to laugh in church!" I get kind of a collective

"Yeah!" from the hearers on this because they are all too familiar with churches that are so hyper serious that laughter is looked upon as inappropriate behavior in a proper church service.

This first joke is one of the best in the book. It is one of those multiple punch line jokes that has three punch lines, each one funnier than the last. By the way, this one requires gestures, so one hand must be free to tell it properly.

The Holy Debate

About a century or two ago, the Pope decided that all the Jews had to leave Rome. Naturally, there was a big uproar from the Jewish community. So the Pope made a deal. He would have a religious debate with a member of the Jewish community. If the Jew won, the Jews could stay. If the Pope won, the Jews would leave.

The Jews realized that they had no choice. They decided to pick a middle aged man named Moishe to represent them. Moishe asked for one addition to the debate. In order to make it more interesting, neither side would be allowed to talk. The Pope agreed.

The day of the great debate came. Moishe and the Pope sat opposite each other for a full minute before the Pope raised his hand and showed three fingers. Moishe looked back at him and raised one finger.

The Pope waived his finger in a circle around his head. Moishe pointed to the ground where he sat.

The Pope pulled out a wafer and a glass of wine. Moishe pulled out an apple.

The Pope stood up and said, "I give up. This man is too good. The Jews can stay!"

An hour later, the cardinals were gathered all around the Pope asking him what had happened. The Pope said, "First I held up three fingers to represent the Trinity. He responded by holding up one finger to remind me that there was still one God common to both our religions. Then I waved my finger around me to show him that God was all around us. He responded by pointing to the ground and showing that God was also right here with us. I pulled out the wine and wafer to show that God absolves us from our sins. He pulled out an apple to remind me of original sin. He had an answer for everything. What could I do?"

Meanwhile, the elated Jewish community had crowded around Moishe, now their hero. "What happened?" they asked.

"Well," said Moishe, "First he said to me that the Jews had three days to get out of here. I told him that not one of us was leaving! Then he told me that the whole city would be cleared of Jews. I let him know that we were staying right here!"

"Yes, yes . . ., and then what???" asked the crowd.

"Well, I don't know," said Moishe. "He took out his lunch and I took out mine!"

Born a Jew, Raised a Jew

A Jewish man moves into a strict Catholic neighborhood. Every Friday the Catholics practically go crazy, because while they're morosely eating only fish, the Jew is in his backyard barbecuing steaks. So the Catholics go to work on the Jew to convert him.

Finally, by long endurance, the Catholics succeed. They take the Jew to a priest who sprinkles holy water on the Jew and intones, "Born a Jew . . . Raised a Jew . . . Now a Catholic!"

The Catholics are ecstatic. No more delicious, but maddening, smells every Friday evening. But come the following Friday, the scent of barbecue wafts throughout the neighborhood once again. The Catholics all rush over to the Jew's house to remind him of his new diet.

They find their neighbor standing over the sizzling steak, knife in one hand, his other hand dipping in a pot of water. He sprinkles water over the meat, saying, "Born a cow . . . Raised a cow . . . Now a fish!"

A Million Years

This curious man was talking to God. He asked God, "How long is a million years in your time frame?"

God said, "Oh, about one second."

Then the man asked, "How much is a million dollars?"

God said, "Oh, about a penny."

So the man said, "God, would you please give me a penny?"

God said, "O.K. Wait just a second!"

The Young Priest

The elderly priest, speaking to the energetic younger priest, said, "You had a good idea to replace the first four pews with plush bucket seats. The front of the church now fills up first." The young priest nodded, and the old priest continued, "And, like you said, we needed a little more beat to the music. Since you brought in that rock 'n roll band, we are packed out."

"Thank you, Father," answered the young priest modestly.

"However," the old priest said, "We need to talk. I'm afraid you've gone too far with the drive in confessional."

"But, father," protested the young priest, "my confessions have nearly doubled since I began that."

"I know, son," said the old priest, "but that flashing sign on the church roof has to go. You know, the one that says, "Toot 'n Tell or Go to Hell!"

Hospital Bill

Mr. Smith arrived at Mercy Hospital by ambulance and was taken right in for open heart surgery. The operation went well, and as the groggy man regained consciousness he was reassured by a Sister of Mercy, who was waiting by his bed.

"Mr. Smith, you're going to be just fine, said the nun, gently patting his hand. "We do need to know, however, how you intend to pay for your stay here. Are you covered by insurance?"

"No, I'm not," the man whispered hoarsely.

"Then can you pay in cash?" persisted the nun.

"I'm afraid I cannot, Sister."

"Well, do you have any close relatives?" the nun questioned sternly.

"Just my sister in New Mexico," he volunteered. "But she's a humble spinster nun."

"Oh, I must correct you, Mr. Smith. Nuns are not spinsters—they are married to God."

A look of relief came over Mr. Smith's face. He said, with a smile, "In that case, please send the bill to my brother-in-law!"

This next joke is a bit more specific than the others. For one thing, the audience needs to know that Baptists, by and large, are teetotalers. This point also came up in the blonde joke about the Singapore Slings. It is also well-known that in this day and age total abstinence from alcohol is not nearly as strong a religious conviction as it once was, even among Baptists. Furthermore, Baptists, generally speaking, are good sports with a better than average sense of humor. All of that makes this a real good joke.

Three Religious Facts

Did you know that there are three absolutely irrefutable religious facts?

Number 1: Orthodox Jews don't recognize Jesus as their Messiah.

Number 2: Protestants don't recognize the Pope as the head of Christianity.

Number 3: Baptists don't recognize each other in the liquor store!

A reason that this joke is so good is that the first two items are very important disagreements among members of some of the larger faiths. Neither one allows for any exceptions to the rule. Listeners are serious and wondering how this could possibly be a joke. The surprise in the third one doesn't begin until half way through the punch line, and it turns out to be a hilarious surprise, even to most Baptists.

One-Liners

Here are some good religious one-liners:

Who was Paul's father?

The thief on the cross because Paul said, "My old man was crucified with Christ!"

What do they call pastors over there in Germany?

German shepherds!

What do you get if you cross a Unitarian with a Jehovah's Witness?

A person who goes from house to house, and doesn't know why!

The Teenage Driver

A teenage boy had just gotten his driver's license. He asked his father, who was a minister, if they could discuss the use of the family car.

"I'll make a deal with you," said his father. "You bring your grades up, study your Bible, get your hair cut, and then we'll talk."

A month later the boy comes back and again asks his father if they can discuss the use of the car.

"Son, I'm real proud of you. You've brought your grades up and you've studied your Bible, but you didn't get your hair cut!"

"You know, Dad, I'd like to talk about that. Samson had long hair, Moses had long hair, and even Jesus and His apostles had long hair!"

"That's right, Son," he replied. "And everywhere they went they walked!"

Temperance Sermon

A southern minister was completing his annual temperance sermon. With great emphasis he said, "If I had all the beer in the world, I'd take it and pour it into the river!"

And then, "If I had all the wine in the world, I'd take it and pour it into the river!"

Finally, the top of his voice: "If I had all the whiskey in the world, I'd take it and pour it into the river!" Sermon complete, he then sat down.

The song leader stood very cautiously, and said to the congregation with a wry smile, "As you can see in your bulletin, our closing hymn is number 239, "Shall We Gather at the River?"

The Nun and the Bedpan

A young nun who worked in home health care started out in the morning for a patient's house. But she ran out of gas.

Fortunately, a gas station was only a block away so she walked over to see if she could borrow a can to put gas into her car. The attendant told her that he had just loaned out his only can, but that it should be back soon.

Instead of just waiting, the nun walked back to her car to assess the situation when her eye fell on a bedpan she was taking to her patient's home. Why not? She decided to take the bedpan to the gas station and get the gas she needed.

As she was carefully pouring the gasoline into her tank, two men on the other side of the street were watching her with amazement. The one said to the other, "If that car starts, I'm joining the Catholic Church!"

Pastor's House Call

The pastor was calling on parishioners, but when he reached this elderly lady's home, no one answered. So, as a friendly and creative gesture, he left his business card in the screen door with "Revelation 3:20" written on it. When she got home, she was supposed to look it up in her Bible and see that it said, "Behold I stand at the door and knock!"

The next Sunday as the pastor was greeting his people after the service, this woman didn't say a word, but pressed a paper into the pastor's hand. When he got home, he saw that the paper only said, "Genesis 3:10." So he got his Bible and looked it up. It said, "I heard your voice in the garden, but behold I was afraid because I was naked so I hid myself!"

He Was a Saint!

In this small town there were these two brothers who had a reputation of being scoundrels. They stole, they cheated, they lied, they were drunkards, they cussed, they chased women, and they spent time in jail.

One of them died and the surviving brother wanted a respectable funeral. He knew it would be hard to get a preacher to do the funeral, so he decided to offer a one thousand dollar honorarium providing the preacher would say that his brother was a saint. There were only five churches in town, and the first four preachers refused to do it. Desperate, he raised the honorarium to twenty-five hundred dollars and approached the fifth preacher with the same stipulation—he had to say that his brother was a saint.

A faint twinkle came into the preacher's eye; and he said that although he had reservations, he would do it providing that the payment came ahead of time. No problem! The brother was greatly relieved.

Surprisingly, a huge crowd showed up for the funeral, not because they wanted to pay respect to the deceased, whom nobody liked, but because they had heard about the deal with the preacher. When the preacher took his place at the head of the casket, he began to preach what a sorry, lowdown, no good, backstabbing, disreputable character the old boy had been all his life. Then as he wound down, everybody gasped when he said, "but compared to his brother, he was a saint!"

The First Confession

A popular Catholic priest was celebrating his 25th anniversary of ministry in a particular town. A large crowd came to the banquet to honor him.

In his address he said, "When I first came to this town 25 years ago I was shocked because the first person who came to me for confession told me a series of terrible sins of immorality, corruption, cheating, and lying. I wondered what kind of people are living in this town. But as the years went by, I found that the people here are wonderful upright and generous people. I love this town and hope to stay here a long while."

After he finished the chief guest, the mayor of the town, arrived. When he took the platform, he said, "I am very sorry to be late, but some urgent matters delayed me at the last moment. The priest and I have been good friends for 25 years. In fact, when he arrived 25 years ago, I was the first person to go to him to confess my sins!"

The Dog Funeral

A man came to the Pentecostal Church and asked to see the pastor. "Pastor," he said, "My dog died and I would like a Christian burial for him."

The pastor said, "I'm very sorry to hear about your dog, but we Spirit-filled Pentecostals don't do funerals for dogs. It's against our theology. You might try the Baptist church down the street. Those Baptists will do almost anything."

The man turned sadly and said, "I'm sorry that you can't do my dog's funeral, but I understand. I'll try the Baptist church. Meanwhile, could you answer a question. I'm not a churchgoer, so I was wondering how much I should leave as a memorial gift for the church. Would $10,000 be adequate?"

"One moment," replied the pastor. "The truth of the matter is that some theological points are quite debatable!"

Hymns and Praise Choruses

An old farmer went to the city one weekend and attended a big city church. When he got back home, his wife asked him how it was.

"Well," said the farmer, "It was good. But they did something different. They sang praise choruses instead of hymns."

"Praise choruses?" said his wife. "What are those?"

"Oh, they're O.K. They're sort of like hymns, only different," said the farmer.

"What's the difference?" asked the wife.

The farmer thought for a minute, and then said, "Well, I'll tell you. It's like this. If I said to you, 'Martha, the cows are in the corn!' well, that would be like a hymn. But if I said to you:

'Martha, Martha, Martha, Oh, Martha, MARTHA, MARTHA,

The cows, the big cows, the brown cows, the red cows, the black cows,

The cows, COWS, COWS are in the corn,

Are in the corn, in the corn, in the corn, in the corn!'

Then if I would repeat the whole thing two or three times, well that would be like a praise chorus."

This is another one of those niche jokes. In order to appreciate it you have to have a background in a traditional church where hymns are used and also in one of the newer churches where contemporary worship is used. Not everyone will see the humor in this joke.

The Wise Mother Superior

The wise old Mother Superior was dying. The nuns gathered around her bed, trying to make her comfortable. They gave her some warm milk to drink, but she wouldn't take even a sip!

So one nun took the glass back to the kitchen. Remembering a bottle of whiskey received as a gift the previous Christmas, she opened it and poured a generous amount into the milk.

Back at Mother Superior's bed, she held the glass to her lips. Mother drank a little, then a little more, and before they knew it she had drunk the whole glass down to the last drop!

"Mother, Mother!" the nuns cried. "Give us some wisdom before you leave us!"

She raised herself up in bed with a pious look on her face and, pointing out the window, she said, "Don't sell that cow!"

The Church Feud

There was this serious feud between the Pastor and the Music Director of the First Baptist Church.

It seems that the first hint of trouble came when one Sunday the Pastor preached on dedicating yourself to full-time service. The Music Director chose to sing, "I Shall Not Be Moved."

Trying to believe that it was just a coincidence, the Pastor put the incident behind him.

The next Sunday, he preached on giving. Afterwards, the choir squirmed as the Music Director led them in the hymn, "Jesus Paid It All."

By this time, the Pastor was more than a little upset. Sunday morning attendance swelled as the tension between the two built and the word got out.

A large crowd showed up the next week to hear the Pastor's sermon on the sin of gossiping. Would you believe it? The Music Director selected the hymn, "I Love to Tell the Story."

The following Sunday, the Pastor told the congregation that unless something changed, he was considering resignation. The entire congregation gasped when the Music Director led them in "Why Not Tonight?"

Truthfully, no one was surprised when the Pastor resigned a week later, explaining that Jesus had led him there and that Jesus was leading him away.

The Music Director could not resist. The closing hymn? "What a Friend We Have in Jesus!"

Wife in Rome

This is another joke I tell on myself so I do not read it.

When you're a seminary professor, you receive some rather strange invitations at times. This one time I got an invitation to an international, interreligious conference that was going to be held in Rome. The foundation would pay all our expenses and spouses were also invited.

We had never been to Rome. So I said to Doris, "Why not? Let's go!"

After we got there and looked at the program we saw that the whole group had been invited to a formal banquet at the Vatican on the second night. I had not noticed this before we left, so I didn't have any clothes for a formal banquet, so Doris and I decided just to go out to some restaurant in the city that night.

But at the coffee break the next morning I was talking to a Jesuit friend I had made, and he asked me if we were coming to the banquet. I told him that I didn't have the right clothes, so we were going to pass. "Look," he said, "I'll tell you what I'll do. Let me loan you one of my clergy shirts, and you can wear it with any suit. That's considered formal dress at the Vatican"

So I thought about it for a minute. "What the heck! Let's do it!"

We got in the hotel room that afternoon and I put it on. It looked pretty good! He gave me a gold cross and I put that around my neck. Then I said to Doris, "The Vatican is right near here and we've got plenty of time. Let's not take a taxi. Let's walk."

So we started off, but we got lost. I approached a policeman to ask for directions. (We are fluent in Spanish, and Spanish speakers can handle a little bit of Italian and vice versa.) He said, "Sure, it's not far. I'll take you there."

Soon we arrived at the elegant door, and I thanked him for guiding us. "Oh, Father," he said. "It was my privilege. Thank you for coming from your country to visit us. If there's anything I can do for you while you're here, just let me know." He gave me his home telephone number and walked away.

I could see that Doris was irritated. When he got out of ear shot, she looked at me and said crossly, "I'm ashamed of you! Don't you realize you deceived that man? Don't you realize that he thought you were a Catholic priest?"

I just looked back at her and said, "Honey, I don't really care at all who he thought I was. But what I'm really worried about is who he thought *you* were!!"

SENIOR CITIZEN JOKES

Some of the best jokes in this book are among the senior citizen jokes, but unfortunately not everybody is qualified to tell them. You might get away with some of them if you are younger, but others tend to be put downs, making fun of things like forgetfulness, sometimes called "senior moments."

However, those of us who are senior citizens ourselves and who have a sense of humor and who don't take ourselves too seriously can have a lot of fun with these jokes. I usually start by saying to my audience, "Ever since I turned seventy—which was quite a few years ago—I have begun to collect senior citizen jokes. Some of them are really good, like this one." I love to start with:

The Drug Store

Henry, age 92, and Nancy, age 89, are all excited about their decision to get married. They go for a stroll to discuss the wedding, and on the way they pass a drugstore. Henry says, "Let's go in."

Henry addresses the man behind the counter"
"Are you the owner?" The pharmacist answers,
"Yes."

Henry says, "We're about to get married. Do you
sell heart medication?"

"Yes, we do."

"How about medication for circulation?"

"All kinds."

:"And medicine for rheumatism and diabetes?"

"Definitely"

"How about Viagra?"

"You bet."

"Medicine for memory problems, arthritis, jaundice?"

"All of the above."

"What about vitamins, sleeping pills, Geritol?"

"Absolutely."

"Do you carry wheelchairs and walkers?"

"All speeds and sizes."

Henry glances at Nancy, then says to the pharmacist, "We'd like to register here for our wedding gifts!"

Here are a couple of quickies which will open the hearers to more senior citizen jokes:

AIDS

Do you know which age group in America is the largest carrier of AIDS? [Pause here for the audience to think about it]

Senior citizens! [Pause again]

Hearing aids! Rolaids! Band Aids! Government aids! Walking aids!

102nd Birthday

I remember when I used to live in Pasadena, California, one woman there was getting ready to celebrate her 102nd birthday. The local newspaper, the *Star News*, sent a reporter to interview her and on her birthday they published an article with her picture.

One of the questions was, "What do you like best about being 102?"

"Oh," the woman said, "Lack of peer pressure!"

Sometimes to establish my credentials and my eligibility to tell senior citizen jokes, I say, "I've been around so long that when I was a kid, the Dead Sea was only sick!"

"Poof" He Got His Wish

This joke is one of the best. It is religious enough to catch the attention of my audiences, and it takes two surprising twists. The first is the husband's request, which does not fit the stereotype of normal missionary desires. This won't provoke a laugh, but rather a quiet gasp. But when the naughty missionary gets his wish, the tension instantly breaks, and people are laughing because they are thinking, "He got just what he deserved!" Here's the way it goes:

There was this wonderful missionary couple in their 60s. They were so faithful to God, they served and sacrificed so much to the Lord, that God decided to reward them here on earth as well as later on in Heaven.

So God sent an angel who told them what a good job they had done, and as a reward God had given the angel authority to grant them any desire of their heart. Anything! The angel encouraged them to think carefully and to ask freely without reservation.

So the wife said, "Sir, I've always wanted to go on an Alaskan cruise."

"Poof!" They were on a cruise!

Then the angel said to the husband, "Now what is your wish?" The husband took the angel over to one side and said quietly, "You know, sir, I've always wanted a wife thirty years younger than me."

And "poof!" He was 90 years old!

Did She Say "Yes" or "No?"

These two senior citizens were living in a Florida mobile home park. She was a widow and he was a widower. They had known one another for a number of years.

Now, one evening there was a community supper in the big activity center. These two were at the same table, across from each other. As the meal went on, he made a few admiring glances at her and finally gathered up his courage to ask her, "Will you marry me?".

After about five or six seconds of careful consideration, she answered, "Yes, Yes, I will." The meal ended and with a few more pleasant exchanges, they went to their respective places.

Next morning he was troubled. Did she say "Yes" or did she say "No?" Try as he would, he just could not recall. Not even a faint memory. With trepidation, he went to the phone and called her. First he explained to her that he didn't remember things as well as he used to. Then he reviewed the lovely evening past. As he gained a little more courage, he then inquired of her, "When I asked you if you would marry me, did you say yes or did you say no?"

He was delighted to hear her say, "Why I said yes, and I meant it with all my heart." Then she continued, "And I'm so glad you called because this morning I couldn't remember who asked me!"

Beautiful and Dumb

I tell this one on myself, so I do not read it. There are places for several audience responses, as I will explain. I start off by saying:

Doris and I have been married 56 years (I change this from year to year, but it is 56 as I write this.). (Sometimes this provokes applause). They've been 56 good years. [pause] Well, most of them have been good! (Laugh)

You know, over 56 years you do have your ups and your downs!

Sometimes when you get in one of those downs, you have a tendency to say something that later on you wish you had never said! (People start nodding agreement)

That happened to me once! (They laugh at the "once")

I said something that later I wish I had never said. You've got to understand that I was really upset! I said, "Sweetheart, I can't understand how God, at the same time, could make you so beautiful and so dumb! (Groan)

So she looked back and me and said, "It's very simple. He made me beautiful so you'd **marry** me. He made me dumb so I would marry **you**!"

Notice the bold words. These are where your emphasis needs to be. I have made the mistake of saying "He made me beautiful so you'd marry **me**," and the whole joke falls flat. It's an excellent example of the need for proper emphasis in telling jokes. It will come with practice.

Holiday Inn

This is a food for thought senior citizen spoof. It is very humorous, but it has a soft punch line. With the poem at the end, however, it will produce a good laugh.

I've done some research. I understand that the average cost for a nursing home is $188.00 per day. There must be a better way to deal with getting old and feeble.

This might be worth a try: I have ascertained that I can get a nice room at the local Holiday Inn for $65.00 per day. That leaves $123.00 a day for food brought to you by room service, laundry, gratuities, and special TV movies. The fee includes use of a swimming pool, a lounge, a washer and dryer, and a business center with computers and a copy machine plus a free breakfast. They provide free shampoo and soap along with toothbrushes, tooth-paste, and razors as requested. I will have daily maid service and a free *USA Today* Monday through Friday. When I do decide to eat in the restaurant, I see different people every day, not the same old fogies that I would see in the dining room of a nursing home. If I join Priority Club, I will soon accumulate enough points to get a DVD player or a free trip to Hawaii.

There may be a bit of a wait to get that first floor room, but that's OK. It takes months to get into a decent nursing home. They have the senior bus, the handicapped bus (if you fake a good enough limp), a church bus, cabs, and even the regular bus. For a change of lunch or dinner, I can take the airport bus and eat in one of the restaurants there.

Holiday Inn has security, and if someone sees you drop over, they will call an ambulance which, in our city, should arrive in 5-7 minutes, about the time it would take to get medical help in a nursing home. They have 24/7 visiting hours. As a bonus, they offer senior discounts. What more can you ask for?

My conclusion?

When I reach those golden years,

Please help me keep my grin.

Just pack my bags and drop me off

At our local Holiday Inn!

What Did I Forget?

An 80-year old couple was worried because they kept forgetting things all the time. The doctor assured them that there was nothing wrong except old age, and suggested that they carry a notebook and write things down so they wouldn't forget. Several days later, the old man got up to go to the kitchen.

His wife said, "Dear, would you get me a bowl of ice cream while you're up?"

"Okay," he said.

"And how about putting some chocolate syrup and a few cherries on it?" she added. "You'd better write it down. Don't forget what the doctor said. You've got your notebook in your pocket."

"Naw," he said. "I won't forget that one."

About 15 minutes later he comes back into the room and hands her a plate of scrambled eggs and bacon.

"Now I told you to write it down," she said, shaking her head in disgust. "I knew you'd forget!"

"What did I forget?" he asked.

She replied, "My toast!"

A Couple Who Always Argued

This couple was getting ready to celebrate their 50th wedding anniversary. They had hung in there together even though they always argued. Day after day, week after week, they were always arguing. Their family knew about it, their friends knew about it...everyone knew they argued.

As the big day was approaching, their grown children did what a lot of families do, they pooled their financial resources to get their parents a really worthwhile golden anniversary gift. They decided to give their parents an all expense paid trip to the psychiatrist!

Well, the parents argued whether they should take the gift; they argued if they should make an appointment, they argued when they should go; they argued about who should drive the car, they argued about what roads to take, they argued in the waiting room, and finally they got to go in and sit in the chairs in front of the desk of the psychiatrist.

The psychiatrist began asking them the normal questions that any psychiatrist asks new patients, but he found out that they argued about the answer to every question. He soon became so frustrated that he decided to take matters into his own hands. He got up, walked around the desk, took the little old woman in his arms, and gave her a big, long kiss right on the lips!

Then he turned to her husband, shook his finger, and said, "She needs that three times a week!"

So the old man scratched his head and slowly said, "Well, Doc, if that's what you say, I guess I can do it. I'll bring her in Mondays, Wednesdays, and Fridays!"

Florida State Trooper

Gordon, who lived in Florida, decided to celebrate his 75th birthday in style. He shoveled out his savings account and traded his Ford Taurus in for a Mercedes convertible.

When he drove it out of the showroom he put the top down and headed for the interstate. 75? He felt like he was 35! Before he knew it, he was doing 80, then 85. He was feeling like he owned the world until suddenly he saw some flashing red and blue lights in his mirror!

No problem. He could take care of this one! So he hit 100, 110, 120. All of a sudden he realized that he couldn't win—the lights were still there! So he pulled over and waited for the trooper.

The officer took a look at this embarrassed senior citizen in a new Mercedes. He said, "Look, this is Friday afternoon and my shift ends in 30 minutes. I'll tell you what. If you can give me an excuse for what you were doing that I've never heard before, I'll let you go with a warning."

Gordon's eyes lit up, and a smile came on his face. He said, "Sir, fifteen years ago my wife left me and ran off with a Florida State Trooper. I thought you were bringing her back!"

The officer said, "Have a good day, sir!"

ETHNIC JOKES

This section on ethnic jokes will intentionally be the shortest one. We live in a politically-correct world in which it is bad taste to stereotype people of any ethnicity, especially when the story makes them look clumsy or stupid. I am appalled when I read old joke books that remind me of how crass and uncouth we used to be. I like the world now, better than the world of fifty or one hundred years ago, at least in this respect.

Humor itself varies from one culture to another. For example, most of us Americans have a hard time understanding why British laugh at something that's not funny and they don't laugh at something else that's really funny. At least according to our American sense of humor.

I have lived for many years outside of the United States, and I continue to travel to other nations several times a year. With the exception of Canada, when I go to other countries I leave my jokes behind. The last two things that can be communicated cross-culturally and linguistically are poetry and humor. My best advice is, don't try. I cringe when I hear fellow American public speakers tell their American jokes in other cultures.

Let me tell you a true story. I have a Korean friend who happens to pastor the world's largest church in Seoul. He frequently invites guest speakers to address his congregation at one or more of his multiple services. One Sunday an American preacher began his sermon with a favorite joke. The pastor, who happened to be interpreting for the speaker that day knew very well that his congregation would not understand the humor in the joke. So, instead of interpreting the words the preacher was saying, my friend would say in Korean after every sentence in English, "Our friend is telling an American joke. . .You will not understand what he says . . .We must be polite and laugh at the right time . . .This will make our friend feel good . . . He is not through with the joke yet . . .But when he is, I will tell you . . .When I say 'laugh,' please laugh hard . . . Pretend that you love his joke!" The American, of course, had no idea what was being said in Korean, but when they did laugh, he was happy, the congregants were happy, and they were all ready for the serious talk.

Here's what I like to do with ethnic jokes:

Hittites

You're not supposed to tell ethnic jokes, because as soon as you tell one, you're bound to hurt someone's feelings. I once said this to a friend of mine, and he was downhearted. He said, "Oh, no! Why did you tell me that? All the jokes I know are ethnic jokes!"

I saw how sad he was, so I had pity on him. I said, "O.K. Look, I'll tell you what to do. Go ahead and tell your jokes, but this time tell them on the Hittites. See, the Hittites went out of existence two thousand years ago, and there are none of them left. So if you tell a joke on the Hittites, you won't offend anyone because there aren't any of them around any more." He really looked relieved, and he said, "Thank you."

A couple of weeks later, I was in the audience and he got up to speak. "Have you heard the one about the two Hittites?" he started. "One of them was named José and the other one was named Manuel!"

The Amish Elevator

This is a kind of ethnic joke, but I tell it anyway. I can't give any logical reason why I tell this joke except that I think it's really a funny joke, it always makes people laugh, and through the years I have not received any negative feedback. So here goes:

An Amish boy and his father were visiting a mall. They were amazed by almost everything they saw, but especially by two shiny, silver walls that could move apart and back together again.

The boy asked, "What is this, Father?"

The father, never having seen an elevator before, responded, "Son, I have never seen anything like this in my life. I don't know what it is."

While the boy and his father were watching with amazement, an old lady in a wheelchair rolled up to the moving walls and pressed a button. The walls opened and the lady rolled between them into a small room.

The walls closed and the boy and his father watched the small circular numbers above the walls light up one at a time. They continued to watch until it reached the last number, and then the lights lit up in reverse order. The walls opened again, and a beautiful 24-year old woman stepped out.

The father, not taking his eyes off the young woman, said quietly to his son, "Go get your mother!"

The only reason I can tell this next one is that I heard it from a Scot. As you will see, only a Scot would be qualified to tell this ethnic joke. So, I'm just reporting what I heard the Scot say:

The Funeral

An Englishman, an Irishman and a Scot had a dear friend who died. At the funeral, they were standing together by the side of the coffin.

The Englishman was sobbing. He said, "I want to show my love!" So he pulled out a $100 bill and put it into the hand of the deceased.

The Irishman said, "Yes, I have the same feeling, but even more." So he pulled out $200 and put the gift into the hand of the deceased.

The Scot, after a long silence, said, "I have never felt so deeply the loss of a friend, so I must demonstrate it as well." He pulled out his check book, wrote a check for $500 and took the $300 as change!"

JOKES ON ME!

When you tell jokes on yourself, especially self-deprecating jokes, you build rapport with your audience. It's possible to overdo this so that it becomes trite and even distasteful, but a little bit of poking fun at yourself is good.

At times I like to use this one, which, by the way, has three punch lines.

Old Stink

When I taught in theological seminary, I attended a Congregational Church. It was a big church of 5,000 members within walking distance of the seminary. Quite often, when a seminary student wakes up on a Sunday morning and doesn't have any other place go to church, he or she will decide to go over to the Congregational Church.

This happened one Sunday. One of the students decided to attend the Congregational Church. He got there just about the time the service was beginning, went down the center aisle, spotted a vacant seat, and as he was settling down into his seat, his eyes cast up on the platform. What he saw there made him say "Aaagh!!" —- loud enough so that the lady who was seated next to him quickly turned her head.

They made eye contact, so he felt obligated to let her in on his little secret. "See that man up there on the platform?" he whispered. She nodded. "That's Old Stink," he said. "Old Stink is one of my professors at the seminary, and I've listened to him five times already this week. If I'd have known that he was going to speak here, I'd have gone somewhere else to church. I don't care to listen to him six times!"

But as he finished, he began to notice a smile curling up on the lips of the lady he was talking to. "Do you know who I am?" she asked. "No ma'am," he replied. "May I introduce you to Mrs. Stink?" (First laugh!)

So he looked back to her and said, "Do you know who I am?" "No," she replied. " Praise the Lord!" he sighed. (Second laugh!)

After a pause: "I never did find out who he was!" (Third laugh!)

Humility Book

Another thing I do to have fun is to play around at our conferences with a book that I happened to write a few years ago with the title, *Humility*. I show them a copy of the book from the platform and say:

I just want to make sure that you don't overlook this book on humility in the bookstore. I'm really proud of this book! (Laugh! Most people think that is the end of the joke, but it isn't.)

Have you heard that my publisher wants to do a new edition? You'll love it. It's going to be a coffee-table sized book with 42 color photographs of me in a variety of humble positions! (Laugh!).

Then they asked me to do a sequel after that one comes out. I've decided to call the new book *The Ten Most Humble Men in the World, and How I Trained the Other Nine!* (Bigger laugh!)

Dying Young?

While you're growing up, there are certain ages that you really look forward to. I can remember that I wanted to be 12, because then I could change from the Cub Scouts to the Boy Scouts.

Then I wanted to be 15 so I could get my driver's permit!

The next one was 21 because then I could vote—you had to be 21 back in those days!

The next was 25 because then my car insurance would go down!

I don't know, I think the next would be 35 because then I would be eligible to be elected president of the United States!

But when that didn't pan out, I kind of lost track, until a couple of years ago, when I realized that I had already reached another one of those ages.

I'm now old enough so that I can't possibly die young!

Why Don't You Do That?

It's true that when you get to be my age, things begin changing, especially the way your physical body functions. It's not the same.

Which reminds me of a while ago when Doris and I were riding on a bus. On the seat across the aisle from us—not right across but a seat or two toward the front—there was this young couple—they must have been in their early twenties—who really loved each other. They loved each other so much that they didn't care who else on the bus knew it. They were really going for it right there in the bus!

When that happens, you try to be polite and to respect their privacy. But you can't help peeking!

After a while, Doris whispered into my ear, "Why don't *you* do that?" [Laugh!]

So I looked back at her and said, "Well, I would. But I don't even know her name!" [Huge laugh!]

MISCELLANEOUS JOKES

These jokes are not particularly related to any of my other categories but I wanted to include them, so "miscellaneous" is probably as good a term as any.

The first one has a long build-up but people don't get bored with it because one, they know for sure that you're going someplace; and two, where you're going becomes less and less obvious with each of the first three people who are thinking about the clandestine kiss. Before the end, the hearers are very curious because it appears to them that all the possibilities have been exhausted, and then, of course, they love the surprise. They are especially happy to see that the corporal, the underdog, manages to put one over on the authority figure in the story.

Slapping the General

Anyone ever been to Europe? [Many hands will go up.]

Anyone ever ride on a train there? [Some will raise their hands again.]

Over there, some of the trains have compartments, and when you sit on one bench you never know who's going to sit facing you on the other bench. [Pause two seconds while they get the scenario.]

This very distinguished and serious general got on a train in Germany. He wore his dress uniform with all his medals and gold braid.

Sitting next to him was a corporal who was his assistant. He made sure the general had reservations for meals, he shined his shoes, he got him coffee, he kept his schedule, he carried his bags, and all those kinds of things.

Before the train left, into the compartment came a beautiful young French girl with her mother. They sat down right across from the general and the corporal.

The train left the station and, like good Europeans, each one sat there minding their own business. Suddenly the train went into a tunnel and everything became black.

After a moment, all you could hear was a kiss and then a slap!

The train came out of the tunnel and all four were sitting there minding their own business.

The mother was thinking, "He kissed my daughter and he got exactly what he deserved!"

The daughter was thinking, "Oh, no! He meant to kiss me, but he kissed my mother!"

The general was thinking, "It's not my day. He gets the kiss, I get the slap!"

But the corporal was thinking, "It's not every day that you can kiss your hand and slap your general!"

Stoplight Picture

Some cities have equipment to take pictures of cars that run stoplights.

In this one city, a man received a ticket in the mail along with a picture of himself in a car, running the red light. The fine was $200.00.

So the man got two $100 dollar bills, took a picture of them, and sent in the picture!

A week later he received a picture of a pair of handcuffs.

He sent the money in!

LET'S LAUGH

Medical Treatment

A woman went to the doctor's office. She was seen by one of the new, young doctors. After about five minutes in the examination room, she burst out screaming and ran down the hall.

An older doctor stopped her and asked what the problem was. After she explained, he told her to sit down and relax.

The older doctor turned and marched straight back to the new doctor with an air of indignation. "What's the matter with you?" he exclaimed. "Mrs. Terry is 63 years old, she has four grown children and seven grandchildren, and you told her right off hand that she was pregnant?"

The new doctor calmly continued to write on his clipboard and said to the older doctor, "Does she still have her hiccups?"

This is usually a delayed reaction response because it takes people a moment to remember that one of the cures for hiccups is supposed to be scaring the person who has them.

174

Wife vs. Husband

A couple drove down a country road for several miles, not saying a word. An earlier discussion had led to an argument, and neither one of them wanted to concede their position. The atmosphere in the car was definitely cold.

As they passed a barnyard full of mules, goats and pigs, the irate husband asked sarcastically, "Relatives of yours?"

"Yep, they are," replied the wife ."In-laws!"

Room 532

Even though this joke doesn't have one of those hilarious punch lines, enough listeners personally identify with the situation described that they have a good laugh over it. You'll like it!

A woman, calling a local hospital, said, "Hello, I'd like to talk with the person who gives information regarding your patients."

The voice at the other end of the line said, "What is the patient's name and room number?"

She said, "Mary Hall in Room 532."

"OK, let me connect you with the nursing station."

"This is nursing station 5-A. How can I help you?"

"I would like to know the condition of Mary Hall in Room 532."

"Just a moment. Let me find her records. Oh, Yes, Mrs. Hall is doing very well. In fact, she's had two full meals, her blood pressure is fine, her blood work just came back as normal, she's going to be taken off the heart monitor in a couple of hours, and if she continues this improvement, the doctor is going to send her home Tuesday at twelve o'clock."

The woman said, "Thank God! That's wonderful! What a relief!"

The nurse said, "It sounds like you must be a family member or a very close friend!"

"Well, not exactly. I'm Mary Hall in 532, and nobody here tells me anything!"

JOKES YOU'RE NOT SUPPOSED TO TELL!

If I don't miss my guess, this will be the first section that a lot of you are turning to. Let me say up front, however, that you read this section at your own risk. Since it is the last section in the book, you can easily take a razor blade and remove it from your copy. No one will know.

Anyone who uses humor soon learns to tailor it according to the audience. Several times I have mentioned that my audiences are usually made up of conservative Christians whose culture has a set of values concerning family, morality, use of language, justice, compassion, prudence, personal dignity, honesty, life, and wholesomeness that attempt to conform to biblical standards and godliness. Consequently, you would expect the jokes in this book to stay within the boundaries of those values.

I agree with those parameters, and I stay within them when I'm telling jokes in public. I try to offend as few people as possible, and by and large I've been successful. At the same time there are some really funny jokes that push the envelope a bit. In my opinion they do not violate Christian principles nor cross the line into blasphemy. They are not sacrilegious. But some of them might poke fun at aspects of sexuality, for example, that the more puritanical of our friends might find offensive. I don't think anyone would rate them X or even R.

One of these is the joke about the Baptist bras that I think is hilarious. I did try this once in public, but afterward I got scolded so badly by my wife as well as through some emails that I never used it again. It is a good example of a joke you're not supposed to tell, at least in public.

The Baptist Bras

A man walked into the lingerie department at Dillard's. He said to the woman behind the counter, " I asked my wife what he wanted for her birthday, and she said to get her three 36B bras."

"What kind?" asked the clerk.

"She said to tell you she wants Baptist bras and that you would know what they are.."

"Baptist bras?" said the woman. "We do have a selection of religious bras, but to be truthful, we don't sell that many Baptists. We sell mostly Catholics, Salvation Army, and Presbyterians."

Confused, the man asked, "What's the difference between them?"

The lady responded, "It's really quite simple. The Catholics support the masses, the Salvation Army

lifts up the fallen, and the Presbyterians keep everything staunch and upright."

"Oh!" said the man. "And how about the
Baptists?"

"Well, they make mountains out of molehills!"

The irony of this joke is that you wouldn't even get it if
you weren't religious and knew something of the characteristics of the different denominations. You have to be aware
that Baptists have the reputation of being among the most
strict in areas of both belief and behavior. If it wasn't a joke
you're not supposed to tell, I would have put it in the section on religious jokes.

By saying that my wife scolded me, I don't mean to
imply that she isn't playful. She does her share of public
speaking, and occasionally she will decide to tell her joke.
She leads up with words to the effect, "My husband tells a
lot of jokes. I have only one, but it's really good. I know that
you might not quite get this joke if you're not as old as we
are, but here it is:

What Happened to Our Relations?

This elderly couple was sitting on the couch
together. All of a sudden, the old man said, "What
ever happened to our sexual relations?"

His wife thought for a moment and replied, "You know, I don't think they even sent us a Christmas card this year!"

Adam and Eve

As we know from Genesis 2, God created Eve from Adam's rib. It says that they were both naked and they were not ashamed.

They apparently were ready for action, but they needed a bit of coaching.

So, God called Adam over to one side, and said, "It's time you got to know Eve a little better. Go over and hold Eve's hand."

Adam came back and said, "That was nice. I like her." God said, "That's good. Now go back and hug her."

Adam said, "Father, what's a hug?" So God explained that he had to put his arms around her, so he went and did it.

Adam returned and said, "That was wonderful. Thank you, Father. Now what?" God said, "Go back and kiss her."

Adam said, "Father, what's a kiss?" So God explained that he had to put his lips on hers, so he went and did it."

Adam returned again and said, "That was unbelievable. Now what?" God said, "Go back and make love to her."

Adam said, "Father, what's making love?" God whispered into his ear and Adam's eyes lit up. He hurried away.

Soon he came back a little more slowly, and said, "Father, what's a headache?"

Eating Ham

Jokes about certain religious taboos are risky. This priest-rabbi joke brings them up, but in such an innocent way that no one is offended except possibly a listener that the implied reference to sex is a bit too explicit. That's why I don't tell it in public.

A Catholic priest and an orthodox rabbi meet on an airplane flight. They quickly establish rapport and begin discussing some of their religious differences. During the conversation, the priest says to the rabbi, "Just between you and me, Rabbi, be honest. Have you ever eaten ham?"

The rabbi blushes, and whispers back, "Confidentially, yes I have!"

A smile comes on the rabbi's face. He says, "Tell me the truth, Father. Have you ever gone to bed with a woman?"

The priest hesitates a moment, then whispers back, "I hate to admit it, but yes, I have!"

"Better than ham, wasn't it?"

The Shy Pastor

The principal of the local girls' high school called the pastor. He spoke to the girls once a year. This year the principal wanted him to speak to them about sex. They agreed to a date and time, but then when the pastor went to note the appointment in his date book, he was a bit shy about writing "girls' high school — sex" because other people had access to his date book. So he decided instead to write "horseback riding."

The day before he was to speak, the principal called to reconfirm. He wasn't home, so his wife happened to answer the phone. His wife said that she could easily go into his study and check the date book.

When she did, she said to the principal, "Yes, no problem—I see that he is planning to be with you tomorrow. However, I 'm not sure about the subject. He's actually only done it twice. The first time he got so sore he could barely walk and the second time he fell off!"

Ronald Reagan's Ducks

One of the biggest joke-telling blunders in modern political history was attributed to Ronald Reagan in his 1980 presidential campaign. He was in New Hampshire, relaxing in a question and answer session, when he told this joke he wasn't supposed to tell:

How do you tell the Polish fellow at a cockfight? He's the one with the duck.

How do you tell who the Italian is at the cockfight? He's the one who bets on the duck!

How do you know the Mafia was there? The duck wins!

This kicked off one of the most massive waves of editorial cartoons in the history of journalism. Poor Reagan was forced to make a formal, public apology within a day. Somehow or other, he still won the election.

Ethan Allen in the Outhouse

Another one of the humor taboos in the audiences I speak to relates to human bodily functions. This is a classic historical joke that I wouldn't tell in public, but I've got to admit, it is one of my favorites. You need to remember that Ethan Allen was one of our great American heroes of the War for Independence from England. The British, to put it mildly, were in bad humor after they lost the war.

It happened that soon after the war was over, Ethan Allen paid a visit to England. The British were making as much fun of the Americans as they could, and they especially had unsavory things to say about George Washington. To needle Allen as much as they could, they found a picture of General Washington and posted it on the wall on the inside of the outhouse that Allen was using.

Someone finally asked Allen if he had seen the picture. Allen said, "Yes, I have. It's a very appropriate place for an Englishman to keep a picture like that."

"Why do you say that?" they asked.

"Very simple," said Ethan Allen. "There's nothing that will make an Englishman [poop—not the real word] so quick as the sight of General Washington!"

The Two Hunters

I haven't told this joke in public, not because of sexual innuendos, but because the misunderstanding is so tragic. However, it is a prize-winning joke, coming up as number one in a poll done by a psychology professor specializing in humor:

These two hunters were out in the woods. A little while after lunch, one of them gasps for air, falls to the ground, stops breathing, and his eyes roll back in his head. His friend shouts to him and shakes him to try to wake him up, but to no avail.

His friend begins to panic, not knowing what to do. Suddenly he remembers his cell phone. He pulls it out, and dials 911. He yells to the operator, "I'm in the woods. My friend is dead! What can I do?"

The operator, in a soothing voice, says, "O.K. Calm down. This has happened before. I can help. I'll tell you what to do, step by step. First of all, let's make sure your friend is dead."

There's a moment of silence, then the operator hears a shot! The guy comes back on the line and says, "O.K. Now what?"

The Mother-in-Law in Israel

Never tell mother-in-law jokes because every audience has a huge number of mothers-in-law who won't like you if you put them down. So I would never tell this religious mother-in-law joke:

A man's mother-in-law was vacationing in Israel. While there, she died in the hotel during her sleep.

The man rushed over and was told that he had two choices for her burial. One, he could bury her there in Israel for $500. Or he could transport her body back to the United States and bury her there, but that would cost at least $5,000.

After thinking about it for a moment, he said that he would take the body back to the U.S. The Israeli officials commented that he must really love his mother-in-law to be willing to spend that amount of money for a decent burial.

He said, "Well, there's more to it than that. I have heard that a long time ago a man that the people didn't like died and was buried there in Israel and that three days later he rose up from the dead. I simply cannot take that chance!"

Converting a Bear

A priest, a Pentecostal preacher, and a rabbi all served as chaplains in a major university. Every week they would get together for coffee and to talk shop.

One day, someone made the comment that preaching to people isn't really all that hard. It would be much harder to preach to a bear.

So they decided to do an experiment. They would all go out into the woods, find a bear, and see who could convert it.

A week later they found themselves in the hospital discussing their experiences.

Father Flannery, on crutches and with a big bandage around his head, says, "Well, I went into the woods to find me a bear. When I found him, I began reading from the Catechism, and he wanted nothing to do with that. He batted me around until I could grab my holy water, sprinkle him and say "Holy Mary Mother of God." When I did, he became gentle as a lamb. Next week the bishop is coming to give him first communion.

Rev. Billy Bob was next. He was in a wheelchair with one arm in a sling and one leg in a cast plus an IV drip. In his best pulpit oratory voice, he said, "Well, brothers, you know I don't have nothin' to do with holy water and sprinklin'. I found me a bear and read to him from God's holy-word. Satan was behind him and he pushed the bear into me. He commenced scratchin' and bitin' until we rolled down the hill into a crick. As soon as we did, I quick dunked him down and baptized him. He became gentle as a lamb and we was praisin' God together.

They both looked down at the rabbi, who was in intensive care with a full body cast and tubes all over. The rabbi glances up and strains to say, "Looking back on it, I've decided that the next time, I won't try to start things out with circumcision!"

Additional copies of this book and other
book titles from DESTINY IMAGE are
available at your local bookstore.

Call toll free: 1-800-722-6774.

Send a request for a catalog to:

Destiny Image® Publishers, Inc.

P.O. Box 310
Shippensburg, PA 17257-0310

*"Speaking to the Purposes of God for this
Generation and for the Generations to Come."*

For a complete list of our titles,
visit us at www.destinyimage.com